Defence Mechanisms in Psychology

A Selection of Classic Articles on the Symptoms and Analysis of Defence Mechanisms

By

Various Authors

British Library Cataloguing-in-Publication Data
A catalogue record for this book is available from
the British Library

Contents

Denial, Other Defense Mechanisms, and the Analytic Process of Cure

Denial

THE INTEREST in elations was revived in the early 1930's when several observers published clinical reports, chiefly of the hypomanic state. Then, principally because of the publication in 1926 of Freud's *Hemmung, Symptom und Angst*,[1] psychoanalysts were particularly interested in recording the defense mechanisms used by the ego to hold the instincts in check and to ward off anxiety. Freud listed those that were prominent in the common neuroses, paranoia, and the depressions. The writers on the elated state commented on another defense mecha-

[1] There are two versions in English of this book, with different titles: a British translation, *Inhibition, Symptom and Anxiety*, and an American translation, *The Problem of Anxiety*. Both are very good.

nism not listed in Freud's book, namely, denial. In 1912, Abraham had remarked that the "manic treats with in-difference the complex" that filled the previous depres-sion; but this statement does not quite declare that the manic state is one that denies external or internal reali-ties. Among the writers on elation, Helene Deutsch (1933) was especially impressed by the importance of denial as a defense mechanism. She stated that denial was the basic defense mechanism in hypomania, and that it played a role there as important as reaction forma-tion in the obsessional neuroses, projection in paranoia and the phobias, or introjection in the depressions.

Quantitatively, there is much to support Deutsch's statement. Denial is certainly the strongest resistance en-countered during the therapeutic analysis of a hypo-manic state. In fact, as a resistance, denial warrants special attention, which it will receive later. As a de-fense, however, denial differs from the ones mentioned above, in that it does not operate directly against in-stinct. "The infantile ego," Freud states (1940), "under the domination of the external world, disposes of un-desirable instinctual demands by means of what are called repressions. We can now supplement this by the further assertion that, during the same period of life, the ego often finds itself in the position of warding off some claim from the *external world* which it feels as painful, and that this is effected by *denying* the percep-tions that bring to knowledge such a demand on the part of reality."

Denial disclaims the external world, then, as repression disclaims the instincts. The repression of instinct, however, is a double matter: there is repression of the idea (the representation, as it is called), and repression of the affect charge, which is the part of instinctual activity that would come to consciousness as an emotion. Then there is also the repression of anxiety, which arises from this buried charge when the ego perceives it as a danger.

Denial may be called upon to help the ego which is in conflict, and it may assist or replace repression. In the discussion which follows, it will be seen that denial is called upon mainly to avoid anxiety; when the instinct representations have become conscious and make a claim on the ego to be accepted as reality (which would be called here "internal" reality, but which can be treated by the ego as if external), denial may make its appearance. There may also be affective denial. Just as there are negations, contradictions, and delusions to offset the intellectual contents, so there may be odd moods, depressions, elations, perplexities, confusions, states of dim awareness, even stupor, which insistently pervade the affective apparatus of the mind (the thymopsyche) and leave no place for anxiety.

Like an instinct, an event (or stimulus) in the external world may be taken as having two aspects: its intellectual representation or idea, and its emotional bearing or impact. Hence, denial may operate like repression in a dual capacity. It may oppose the intellectual recognition of an external fact, say a death, and state that it did not occur, and this may lead to a negative or positive delusion. Or it may oppose the affective impact of the external fact; although admitting that a death did occur, the ego's point of view would be that it did not matter. In the elations we shall find that it is chiefly this aspect of denial—the denial of the emotional impact of reality—which influences the clinical picture.

Hence, it will be seen at once that though denial may fairly be compared to the defenses that operate directly against instinct, and serves as they do to settle conflicts between ego and id, or ego and superego, the *modus operandi* is very different. The effect of denial is to rupture the intellectual rapport or emotional attuning of the ego with its environment. As Freud says, denials are, for the most part, half measures, incomplete detachments from reality. "The rejection is always supplemented by an acceptance; two contrary and independent attitudes always arise and this produces the fact of a split in the ego. The issue again depends upon which of the two can command the greater intensity."

Deutsch succeeded in analyzing the central latent fact that was denied by her patient's chronic hypomania. The patient was denying that she lacked a penis, and from this central latent denial irradiated a host of manifest secondary ones. "During the time that she was in analysis," Deutsch wrote (1933), "her husband and lover both deserted her, she lost most of her money, and she experienced the melancholy destiny of mothers whose growing son deserts them for another woman. Finally, she had to accept the narcissistic blow of my telling her that she could not become a psychoanalyst. None of this was capable of disturbing her euphoria. She immediately found a way out, partly by belittling her losses, partly by finding at once new substitutes; thus she nipped in the bud any reaction to her frustrations and denied them."

Other Mechanisms in Elations

The prominence of denial in the prolonged hypomanic state did not obscure for Deutsch the presence of other defense mechanisms, which, theoretically considered, are possibly of equal utility. Thus, in the hypomanic state there was a period of *projection,* in which all manner of aggressive intentions were attributed to the analyst. There was also much *identification* during the happier periods, seen as direct efforts to compensate for a loss. The pith of this is given by a reference to another of Deutsch's patients, who was forced to interrupt her analysis because of the analyst's vacation and traveled under the assumed name, "French." In a euphoric state she told strangers fantastic stories about herself; the stories contained such facts as she knew about Dr. Deutsch. A duplicate of this observation occurred in my own practice: while I was on vacation, a patient developed a hypomanic attack, and the colleague who saw her then was struck by her imitation of my gestures and mannerisms, such as my style of smoking.

In the brief hypomania, reported by me in 1932, which lasted seven days, I noted much denial in dreams, fantasies, and particularly in the transference reactions. Quite justifiable remarks about the patient were taken as proof of the other person's "evil mind." Thus her parents' realistic suspicion that she was having an affair provoked her indignant comment, "They would think that," as if it were an incredible and unsupported opinion. The mildest repetition to her, in paraphrase, of what she had been saying provoked sarcastic retorts— "That's what you analysts think." And in her dreams, true statements, whether of external fact or critical of herself, were put in the mouths of people she need pay no attention to, for example, a paranoid woman. In fact, her dreams were instructive in showing how denial gains oneiric representation. Things to be repudiated were portrayed as games, as theatrical or cinematic perform- ances, as parts of a work of fiction, or as the statements of drunken, insane, or mendacious persons. In short, the unpleasant was in one way or another declared to be a lie or a fiction. It was not always possible semantically to distinguish denial from projection; the two defenses often co-operated.

On the other hand, the identifications were extremely prominent. After a transference frustration, which arose when she eavesdropped on the analyst and another female patient, and a day of being morose and rude, she entered a mild elation that repeated a "primal scene" or infantile observation of coitus. In the hypomania, she acted both parental roles and the role of an observing baby (a younger sibling) to boot. She described among other things a sort of hypomanic coitus. Relating her feelings during intercourse with her former lover, a much respected superego figure, she spoke of a fusion of their two personalities and identities, each entering the other and becoming part of the other, the union being perfect when he took her breast in his mouth during orgasm. This union she likened to a mutual nursing, and in fellatio foreplay, she thought that the penis must have the same relative proportions for her as an adult that the nipple would have for a baby at the breast. The feeling of being one with her lover gave her a sense of partaking in his qualities, as part of him, like membership in a cause of large social or religious import, woman's suffrage or the Church; and her language was reminiscent of that used by mystics in describing their transports and sense of fusion with God—for example, Saint Teresa. The lover stood for God and the breast at the same time, and the case neatly illustrated Rado's remark that in mania the ego fuses with its superego in an accurate intrapsychic reproduction of the fusion of baby and breast at nursing.

Along with denial, in this short elation there appeared very prominently the defense mechanisms of identification, projection, and rapid alternations of activity and passivity. Together, and considering the ego-superego fusion, they impressed me particularly as proving that the patient's "hypomanic ego" was what Freud had described as a "purified pleasure-ego," which included within it all its superego figures, regressively eroticized in a way that exactly reversed the process by which the superego is formed.[2] Freud defines the pleasure ego as an early organization dominated by the pleasure princi-

[2] "This superego . . . originated through the introjection into the ego of the first objects of the libidinal impulses in the id, namely, the two parents, by which process the relation to them was desexualized, that is, underwent a deflection from direct sexual aims."—Freud (1924)

ple, before the maturing ego has definitively put itself under the guidance of reality testing and conscious judgment, and before superego formation. The attainment of pleasure and avoidance of unpleasure is the sole criterion of acceptability for the pleasure ego. Speaking of the *anlage* or matrix in the pleasure ego from which the function of judgment is later evolved, Freud says: "Expressed in the language of the oldest instinctual impulses, that is, the oral ones, the alternative runs thus, 'I should like to eat that, or I should like to spit it out.' "

Denial, therefore, as a defense fell into a certain context. It was, for my patient literally (her elation included many direct, expulsive, mouth symptoms), as for elations in general, a function of the pleasure ego, and with the other defenses, indicated this early type of ego organization. In my paper, therefore, I was led to emphasize this particular aspect.

Hypomanic Characters and Neurotic Personalities: Diffuse Denial

A suffusion of the whole personality by the mechanism of denial led Anny Angel (1934) to refer to two patients as chronic optimists. Despite only too much evidence to the contrary, these women believed that everything would inevitably come out right in the end. Disregarding extraordinary frustrations in fact, they were able to think only of unavoidable happy endings and preserved an entirely unwarranted, even dangerous, cheerfulness. In both cases, in the unconscious, the happy ending meant the ultimate acquisition of a penis. From this root, their "never say die" attitude spread to most parts of their personality. In a comparable male case in my practice, the denial was of masculinity and was anchored in a strong identification with the mother.

Closely related to the chronic optimists are the "neurotic hypomanic personalities," whom I described (1937) and named thus by analogy with the neurotic depressions and "neurotic characters." Along with many neurotic symptoms, either conversion or obsessional, these persons are characterized by the immense enterprise they show in daily affairs, overfilling their time with inconsequential doings, throwing themselves vigorously into hobbies, sexual affairs, or business deals, to drop them all abruptly with a striking sudden loss of interest. Their analysis shows a latency period in which strong identifications are built up with a usually dead or absent parent, and a sharp, often conscious recrudescence of incestuous wishes at puberty, followed by a vehement plunge into activities as a distraction. Along with the overactivity, neurotic symptoms of various kinds develop, of which the most constant is insomnia. In their analysis, the discovery of painful data is avoided or bagatellized, and countered by "hypomanic" acting out instead of working through.

A special type which I described (1941) as *hypomanic obsessional neurosis* shows predominantly a typical obsessive symptomatology. But in contrast to the general run of obsessional patients, these patients are prevailingly cheerful and optimistic and a little plus in affectivity. Instead of distracting themselves and buttressing their denials by action, like the preceding type, the patients escape by attacking interpretations with wit and humor, but of a strangely "dead pan" type. Their response is to pay attention to the word rather than the sense of what is told them and to play semantically with puns and rhyme. Snatches of song may appear in their associations, hymns or popular ditties, yet more to entertain the analyst than to express pleasure. Their denial mainly attacks being told and having their fantasies interfered with. Wit, an ego mode which carries much aggressive cathexis to a discharge, and which may be pleasurable in itself, is here impressed by the ego into the service of affective obsessional resistance, with very little pleasure premium, consciously, for the patient. (See Kris, 1950.)

Denial in Severe Manic Excitement

In the cases reported by the authors mentioned above, denial as a defense mechanism was seen at work in what were, clinically speaking, mild elations, in that they were capable of psychoanalytic treatment. In a hospitalized case of a severe "circular psychosis," Almasy (1933) took shorthand notes of manic flight. He found that the verbal productions were far from free associations. He stated in a preliminary report, which unfortunately was not followed up, that the talk was rigid (*gebunden*), that all painful themes were eliminated, that distractions accounted for most of the contents and at the same time made them quite irrelevant and empty (*verödet*). The patient's speed prevented her or anyone else from understanding what she meant, and this dodge kept her away from her real troubles. The shorthand notations permitted Almasy to find traces of important matter in her productions. She was keeping her mind away from the fact that she was ill and unfit for work and needed a surgical operation badly; that her husband was gravely, perhaps fatally ill; and that her family was in a most precarious economic situation. Almasy treated her by somehow getting her to focus her attention on him and then explaining to her the unconscious meaning of her remarks about him. She recovered without a satisfactory understanding of her condition and was discharged before Almasy could check up or continue his study.

The material of the grave manic attacks has not been deeply studied from the point of view of the defenses. Early reports, such as Campbell's (1914), Dooley's (1921), and MacCurdy's (1913), could point to trends and even suggest unconscious material, but like Almasy's, they had to stop short almost at the precipitating situation. However, a glance at most manic histories, as they appear in an ordinary hospital report, will show that the manic attack is a denial of just such precipitating situations as we have come, in psychoanalysis, to regard as revivers of childhood conflicts and frustrations. Prominent among the precipitants of manic attacks is childbirth, a fact to which psychiatrists often attribute the statistically higher incidence of women among the manic-depressive patients. (Lange, 1928; but see Gerö's more profound explanation, cited in Chapter 2.) The puerperal manias are usually excited affirmations of virginity and denials of marriage and motherhood, and they readily permit inferences as to the unconscious conflicts, even without psychoanalysis. Most severe manias obviously repudiate precipitating events, and it is plausible that a deeper study, if it could be made, would show links between the precipitating events and infantile conflicts, comparable to those that join adult female sexuality with the infantile in the puerperal manias.

It is generally recognized that elation is an unstable defense (Deutsch, 1933; Klein, 1935). Its presence in an otherwise schizophrenic setting is used by psychiatrists as a prognostically good sign. The question in such indeterminate elations is to what extent the ego's break with reality is maintained by denial alone (or predominantly) with the elated mood offsetting the appropriate affect charge. A study of the various kinds of breaks with reality, ranging from transient denials through severe "world destruction," has only begun.

Denial in Ego Development

As the preceding survey shows, denial takes a high place among the defenses in the psychology of the elated states, though not an exclusive one. Considered genetically, denial and the other defenses are seen to be functions of a special ego structure, the pleasure ego, which rules in elations and elated states. In an adult, the appearance of the defense mechanism, denial, indicates that there has been a regression of some degree to this stage of ego development, of which it is an intrinsic and essential function. Denial stands, so to say, at the boundary of the pleasure ego, repelling external realities or any psychic realities that can plausibly be treated as if they were external.

The growing child's ego is more nearly a pleasure ego than is an adult's, and it is due to the child analysts, particularly to Anna Freud (1936), that we possess some insight into the mechanism of denial. The child, not stringently bound to the reality principle, plays and imagines, and its moods and feelings are determined to a greater or less degree by its games and fantasies. It easily denies realities that surround it, and denial as a defense mechanism plays a role in its normal life as well as in the childhood neuroses. According to Anna Freud, the prominent conflicts in the child are between the instincts and the external world, and its ego finds little difficulty in accepting an altered view of the latter.

Anna Freud's discussion of Freud's analysis of Little Hans (1909) is relevant to the problem of elation, for it illustrates how a denying fantasy produced a *good humor*. Five-year-old Hans had displaced his unconscious aggression against and fear of his father onto horses, and feared that horses would bite him. His analysis cured him of his phobia by destroying the defenses against instinct, such as displacement and repression, but it left him in an unsatisfied frame of mind, for he had been made to realize that he was too small to compete successfully with his father for his mother's love, and he also knew that he could not share in the care his mother was expending on his little sister. This bad external situation was not to his liking and so he fantasied, denying it: the plumber came and fitted him out with large genitalia, and he had lots of babies to bathe and take to the toilet. These fantasies, Anna Freud emphasizes, raised Hans's spirits; they put him in a good humor, a mood dependent therefore on his capacity to deny his real frustrations by means of his imagination.

Other little boys, described by Anna Freud, escaped the development of phobias by denying their real weakness and incompetence through fantasies in which they figured as strong and powerful beings, such as menagerie owners and lion tamers. Still other children did not limit their denial of reality to pure fantasy, but bolstered their repudiations by words and actions. A little boy, whose oedipal conflict caused him to be anxious in the presence of grown men, took to wearing a cap with a stiff brim to counterpoise his inferiority, and he wore this cap even at meals and in bed. A little girl, mortified by her lack of a penis, continually pointed to things that did not exist, saying for example, "Look. The hen laid an egg," and disappointing the siblings that believed her.

Anna Freud remarks that in early childhood denial through fantasy ordinarily has no lasting effect. Continued into the latency period, it may lead to general alterations of character, such as lying or an exaggerated facetiousness and disinclination to be serious, and in adults it can hardly exist to any important extent except in a psychotic frame. To commentate on these remarks as to their bearing on the matter of obtaining or preserving good humor and emotional balance, or elation generally, it might be said that it becomes progressively harder with age and growth to "split" off a pseudo reality that is controlled purely by the pleasure principle. The psychotic frame to which Anna Freud refers includes such a split. A normal adult ego must settle its conflicts usually by a defense directed against the instincts, and denial and fantasy can play but an insignificant part.

Denial in Sleep and Dreams

Anticipating some of the contents of a later chapter, I should like to point out that there is a normal split in the psyche, persisting through life, in which denial of reality may come to full fruition, namely, sleep and the dream life. The institution of the bedtime story recognizes the approaching split with daytime realities. Though unsatisfactory for any long-term solution, sleeping and dreaming possess the advantage of temporarily excluding external reality and often inner, psychological factors. Particularly in children, according to Freud (1900), where dreams are apt to be direct and undistorted wish fulfillments, frustrations and ungratified anticipations of the previous day may be denied in fantasy. In later years, it is true, dreams may yield little conscious, manifest satisfaction, and many adult dreams contain too many ego elements and too much censorship for this purpose. But dreaming represents fantasy that is taken away and split off from the ego's complete control and from everyday influences.

The wish to sleep, then, needs consideration in a psychoanalytic account of a state, such as elation, which is an attempt at autarchic affective regulation—a jerry-built, synthetic effort to preserve good humor and self-regard. It would seem a priori that an adult, set upon denial, might simply turn to sleep and dreams, where the existence of external facts is denied and the emotions are replaceable by their opposites or easily obscured by vagueness and dullness. It is thus that a child turns to his daytime imaginations, and others to music or other emotional replacements. For an adult this turning to sleep and dreams is not a simple procedure, and a chapter on mania and sleep will consider some of the difficulties. It is worth mentioning here that in some psychoses or stages of a psychosis (Brunswick, 1928; Freud, 1941), waking life may be delusional and divorced from reality, while the dream life is "sane" and attuned to the truth.

Fetishism

A nonpsychotic split, according to Freud (1928, 1940), enables the fetishist to maintain two realities, specifically in regard to the existence of the female penis. Out of castration anxiety, the fetishist refuses to recognize the fact that women have no penis, because this would be evidence that "castration" in general might exist and that he ran the chance of being castrated. Freud states (1940): "He therefore rejects the perception of his own senses, which showed him that women's genitals lack a penis, and holds fast to the opposite conviction. The rejected perception, however, does not remain entirely without effects, for, in spite of everything, the patient has not the courage to assert that he really saw a penis. He snatches hold of something else instead—a part of the body or some other object—and attributes to it the role of the penis which he cannot do without." This is not a split, but: "Now we come across fetishists who have developed the same dread of castration as non-fetishists and react to it in the same way. Their behavior, therefore, simultaneously expressed two contrary presuppositions. On the one hand they are denying the fact that they have perceived that women's genitals lack a penis; and on the other hand they are recognizing the fact that women have no penis and drawing the right conclusions from it. The two attitudes persist side by side through their whole lives without affecting each other. Here is what may rightly be called a split in the ego."

Unfortunately, so far the study of fetishism has not afforded us assured knowledge about the relationship of this condition to the more general ego problems and the emotional states that interest us here.

Denial as Resistance

As Freud has shown, the ego's defenses are discernible by the analyst because of the resistances that the patient's ego puts up against the psychoanalytic work. The defenses are best studied when they appear as resistances during therapeutic analysis, for then their relationship with the instincts, with the superego, and with the external world are easily subjected to analytic scrutiny and testing. Indeed, the surest knowledge that analysts have about the ego has been gained thus, and the study of the resistances is still the cardinal step in analytic exploration of the ego. (See Anna Freud, 1936.) In the 1920's analysts were not so alive to this point, and the theory of the ego was handled mainly in accord with conceptions of its topography and economy, and not of its defenses. Hence, Freud's early remarks about denial lay clinically fallow for some years before their significance was appreciated.

Although the idea of defense is closely tied up with the idea of resistance, the latter term has connotations of its own which justify a separate consideration of the use of denial as resistance. Denial appears as a defense mechanism in the elated states and serves to elucidate them. But it appears also as a resistance during the analysis of neurotic and relatively normal persons; in fact, it is sometimes set into action by the analytic process, and similarities between the denials encountered in the "natural" elations and those that are the product of analytic technique deserve some special notice. Not only does such notice aid in the clarification of certain features of the manic states, but also, ideas that come from the study of the elations contribute to the theory of analytic technique.

Analytic Process and Affective States

The natural clinical "course" of a depression or elation has some points in common with a therapeutic analysis. This thought arises from several comparisons that Freud and others have made between mourning and analysis, particularly of the part of the analytic process known as "working through," a technical term which designates a patient's accepting and assimilating the truths that are discovered by interpretation and free association.

Freud (1925) devoted a special study to an attitude that many analytic patients demonstrate, which he called *negation*. When the patient is given a certain interpretation or comes to a conclusion about the meaning of a piece of analytic material, he enters a demurrer. "You'll think I mean to insult you, but I really have no such intention," runs one of Freud's examples. Or: "You ask me who the person in the dream might be. It was not my mother," which, Freud says, we may emend: So it was his mother. The patient had thought of his mother in connection with the figure in the dream, but he did not want the association to count. Similarly, an obsessional patient will have a new obsession, hit upon its meaning at once, and then proceed to rationalize it away. Negation, in short, is a way of knowing what is in repression. The repressed may enter consciousness as an idea, but on condition that it be set aside intellectually. The emotions appropriate to the idea remain repressed. The patient knows an idea but he does not feel its validity and relevance to his person.

Discovery of the intellectual content while the emotion is still repressed, as described above, is a familiar and important situation in analytic therapy. (See Benedek, 1937.) In the days of catharsis, no such gap was present between insight (with recovery of buried ideas) and the emotional release. But in a present-day psychoanalysis at this particular point, we are alert for an ego reaction, either an attempt at defense or assimilation. The patient might, for example, respond to his insight with an aggravation of symptoms; that is, he might have a so-called negative therapeutic reaction, which, as Gerö (1936) remarks, characterizes the analysis of persons with depressions. Or, conceivably, the emotional pressure might seek an outlet in some new symptom or in an "acting out" in some life theater, which would attempt to confirm or deny the interpretation or insight. Of this acting more will be said, for it may take a form that is by no means a direct instinctual expression; it may indeed be a denial in action of the very emotion in question and not a spill-over. Another path the analysand might take, ideally, is that of recasting his judgments, agreeing intellectually with the new idea and immediately accepting it emotionally, which would be tantamount to a quick working through. The appropriate affect would then appear in consciousness even though it might be preceded by some bad quarter hours of anxiety.

"Technical Elation"—A Screen Affect

No special mood need accompany the phenomenon of negation. In the case of a fairly indifferent thought, particularly in an experienced analysand, the mood might remain relatively neutral. But, beyond this, in possibly every analysis, there are negative periods or moments of denial in which this is not the case. The denial is not limited to conscious negative judgments or contradictions, but appears as a general reaction. In company with the intellectual repudiation and repudiative actions, an elation emerges and dominates the patient's state of mind. I have noted this "technical" hypomania, i.e., elation evoked by analytic technique, in many patients. It is a counterpart of the transient depressed mood that may appear during an analysis when the facts that are uncovered offend the patient's narcissism. A manic's flighty, dispersed attention to the environment fills his consciousness and excludes or crowds into a corner facts and topics that would trouble him or pain him. Similarly, the elation produced by the psychoanalytic technique—the euphoria that accompanies the denial—leaves no room for other affects, particularly not for anxiety. Thus, to amplify Freud's remarks, whereas denying words and negative acts of judgment deal solely with the intellectual content of the repressed, the elated mood, serving the repressing forces and the ego's defense, deals with the emotional content or threatened anxiety.

Of the mild hypomania which occurs as part of a therapeutic analysis, I stated (1941) that it could be observed "concomitantly with or immediately subsequent to the successful resolution by analysis of neurotic symptoms which have been used as a defense," and I gave a brief example. The symptom was an airplane phobia of an unusual type. The fear was not connected with any idea of falling or heights but was brought about simply by a plane ride and appeared only during the plane's motion. The patient would sit with her eyes tightly closed till the landing relieved her anxious tension. Through dreams it was learned that the airplane was a reminder of an upstairs sleeping porch which the patient had shared as a child with her parents. The excitement of the plane ride reproduced the excitement she had experienced on that porch as an involuntary third party anticipating her parents' sexual behavior. Of importance clinically, when she became aware of these connections intellectually, she grew restless and playful, and in the analytic hour for some days she showed an elevation of mood quite out of keeping with her usual quiet behavior and unhappy mood. Only after this brief elated period could she encompass the emotional events, aggressive and erotic, as they were lived originally on the sleeping porch.

Now, as Freud remarked, the knowledge of what was repressed, such as my patient possessed, implies only that the intellectual content was removed from repression. The aggressive and the erotic feelings that repeated those which she had had on the porch were not immediately remembered, and her elation was an affective resistance to the feeling memories of that past time. It is of course true that affects may be accurately reproduced in analysis, but equally obviously, whatever moods emerge then may not duplicate the original childhood feelings but some that came later. They might, to stretch an analogy, be called *screen affects*, in that they present themselves to hide others. Indeed the comparison with screen memories holds in several ways: the screen memory is a "real" memory that conceals another real memory; it deceives as to chronology. Similarly, the screen affect feels real, but it conceals another real feeling, and it is also wrong in regard to the time of occurrence. (See Green-acre, 1949.)

We may, for example, let ourselves imagine that Little Hans is being analyzed as an adult and that he has re-called his fear of being bitten by a horse. He comes to see that the horse must stand for his father; however, he says, "It can't really be so." To imagine further, with-out overtaxing our invention, while Hans is in this hypo-thetical state of negation, he fantasies or recalls the fantasy that the plumber intervenes beneficently and equips him with large genitalia. This idea is accompanied by the pleasure and *good humor* that went with it in childhood; that is, in technical terms, Hans has an ana-lytically produced, resistant elation. After this resistance and good humor, which repeats his childhood "denial through fantasy," Hans may begin to remember the sexual and aggressive oedipal feelings that preceded the horse phobia.

In neurotic hypomanic characters, where the analysis often runs from one elated denial to another, the de-fensive nature of the elation is definite. After a trans-ference disappointment or a repetition in real life of an oedipal defeat, into which the patient has intellectual insight, there is a persistent unwillingness to feel pain for the loss or frustration. Instead, banal, trivial "nice things" happen, people seem to have entered into a con-spiracy to do the patient good, and his analysis is very entertaining. His good spirits bar from memory the original infantile feelings; and as his mood appears to be a screen affect, so his attention is filled with details of the type usually chosen for innocuous screen memories. The acceptable feelings are analogous to acceptable memories.

To deny his previous story of an unhappy childhood, a "schizoid manic" personality (*sit venia*) in an elation told me obviously fantastic stories that completely contradicted his first account. He had been, he said, the darling of his parents and siblings all through childhood and adolescence; he had been very popular at school and had made many wonderful friendships. My reminder that he had told me quite a different story, one of great frustration, shyness, and seclusiveness, was almost shouted down. That was all wrong, he said, his analysis was bringing back to him the true memories of his childhood, which he had forgotten, and he would thank me not to interfere now while he was recovering them. The "forgotten memories" had all the banality of the usual screens.

Elation an Interruption to Analysis

As a resistance during analysis, elation is seen to represent a defense against reality and against the effective admission of known dangers, losses, rejections, and defeats. It appears as an interruption of the analytic process, an inappropriate substitute for working through, and not as the termination of analytic work. Hence, it is difficult to agree with Abraham's suggestion that the prototype of mania in normal persons is the feeling of well-being and energy, which the author noted after normal mourning. In a point-by-point comparison of the events of mourning and melancholia-mania processes, mania would be the "opposite number" of an interruption of the work of mourning and not a state where the libido is truly freed from the lost object. In the elation, the grief work is temporarily laid aside, insight is suspended, and the object relationship denied in respect of its emotional meaning. The naïve formulation that mania is an escape from depression is a specious insight into this quality of the elation. It expresses the thought that the depression is by no means over, but it ignores the interruptive nature of the exalted mood. Elation in fact represents a different defense than depression qualitatively and not a diminution in the defensive efforts. Empirically, my own cases, as well as those reported by Deutsch (1933) and Klein (1940), demonstrate the validity of the idea that elation interrupts and does not terminate the process analogous to mourning. The apparently terminal elation puts aside the depression, which comes to light again later.

To turn the matter around, a manic patient is like a person caught for a time in an incomplete analysis, specifically, like someone halted at the moment of denying an idea or perception, or one who is avoiding its emotional consequences in a mood that varies from good humor to exaltation.

Analytic Working Through and the Grief Work

In "Mourning and Melancholia," Freud permits a comparison of the working-through process in mourning or depression and the process of the same name which refers to a part of analytic therapy, and he returns to this topic in *The Problem of Anxiety*. Both in mourning and in analysis, the working-through period is a time of reality testing, a function which is disturbed in mania. In analysis the discovery of events and impulses that led to the formation of a neurosis is not sufficient for a cure. The analysand still has to subject many related manifestations to new inspection and with better understanding pass conscious judgment on the many facts that make up his maladjustment. A retraining in correct emotional appreciation is accomplished usually by means of "reliving" or re-experiencing events subjectively in the transference relationship, which comes to be understood and felt as "unreal" and as a repetition of obsolete impulses and attitudes. As Freud remarked in his criticism of Rank's going "straight to the core," simply to throw out the burning lamp that started the conflagration does not put out the fire.

Fenichel credits Rado with priority in pointing out the similarity of the reality testing in the analytic process of working through and the work of mourning.[3] As to melancholia, Freud considers that it differs from normal grief in that the analogue of the grief work takes place in the unconscious and affects only the representations in the system Ucs. Leaving aside the matter of working through in melancholia, Rado (1925), as well as Alexander (1925, 1927), made use of the current ego psychology, based on the theory of depressions, to sup-

[3] Fenichel, 1941, p. 50, and 1945, p. 572. I fail to find the simile attributed to Rado in the reference that Fenichel gives (Rado, 1925), but Rado has used it in lectures.

port theories of analytic technique and therapy. Figuratively, we might say that a mourner is in analysis with his superego, trying to come to terms with his superego's conceptions of his character and behavior. The analytic patient was shown to be ascribing a superego role to his analyst in the transference situation, and Alexander outlined a theory of what went on in a therapeutic analysis, a metapsychology of analytic therapy, which in effect showed the parallel between the mourning process and the process of analysis. Stress was laid on the economic and topographic consequences of the transference, the superego role ascribed to the analyst, and the deflection outward, during analysis, of sadism from its inward, ego-directed path. Cure took place by the same dynamic means as recovery from a depression or grief.

The differences and similarities between grief and the analytic process are worthy of mention. In both, the ego tests reality gradually and piecemeal, but with some difference in the conception of reality. In fact, in depressions there is consciously not so much a reality testing as a morality testing. The ego is not trying to separate the true from the false but the good from the bad. When, therefore, in ordinary analysis the id striving is preconscious and accepted intellectually ("It seems from this that I must have wanted father to die"), the cathectic bounce of the striving is by no means diminished. Between the intellectual discovery and the emotional acceptance, during the time of reality testing between the "so it seems" and the "so it is" come the very mood

alterations that saturate the psyche in the psychotic elations and depressions.

Between mourning and analytic working through,
there is often more than a mere analogy, for mourning
may appear in the course of an analysis as part of the
working through. The negative therapeutic reaction, for
example, that follows a piece of intellectual insight is
the work of the superego and the equivalent of a depression (Gerö, 1936); it often covers anxiety about loss
of love. Elation which follows intellectual insight is a
denial. Though the patient may obligingly repeat back
his "insight," his denial will be expressed in his mood
and actions. When it was said in the past that a patient's
narcissism sets a limit to analytic therapeutic efforts, the
reference was in part to these affective reactions. That
type of acting out which contradicts the analysis and
its findings is often a variety of manic denial through
activity. In short, many of the resistant manifestations
of an analysis may be fitted into the course of an affective disorder or be taken as part of a process of mourning.

Analytic and "Natural" Elations

To be in earnest about the theory that elation is an
unterminated analysis caught in an interrupted period
of working through, it may be pointed out that life
often plays the analyst and gives people "interpretations," in the form of facts and ideas which they realize
are true with their intellect but to which they cannot
commit themselves emotionally. The acceptance of such
realities entails a subsequent emotional catching up, like

the grief work, and this may be interrupted, interfered with, or countered by a denial, a refusal to accept, of which the emotional component is an elation. The denial may take the forms described by Anna Freud for children: denial with fantasies, or denial through words and deeds that produce good humor and are brought in to oppose the unwelcome and unavoidable reality. The elated patient acts out his denial and lengthens or postpones his working through.

Normal Mourning and Instinct Alteration

The merits and defects of mourning as a psychotherapy are self-evident. If it were a therapeutic process, it would have a very limited aim—the solution of a specific object relationship. Permitting the superego to play the part of the analyst also limits insight and sets an obsolete standard of reality. Conscience and conscious judgment compete. As in the neo-Latin languages, where the words for *conscience* and *consciousness* are the same, there is a great risk of confusion. Historically, years of moral self-judging preceded objective self-judging, both in the race and the individual. Yet, mourning brings self-judging and introspection too, and it has not been sufficiently appreciated how much normal mourning may increase insight into the self. The mourner submits his relationship with the departed object to intellectual review and gains new insight into his emotional needs and dependencies. Reflection concerning the lost object, which is part of the normal grief work, leads to knowledge about the mourner's self and motives. Such reflection may indeed be considered a sublimation of the oral sadism that gets expressed in its native terms in the melancholic, primitive form of mourning.

Indeed, in his paper on "Negation," Freud shows how conscious judgment, as a function of the ego, is derived from earlier instinctual, oral action. "Judgment," he writes, "has been systematically developed out of what was in the first instance introduction into the ego or expulsion from the ego, carried out according to the pleasure-principle." And previously in the same paper, he remarks of the early forerunner of judgment: "Expressed in the language of the oldest, that is, oral instinctual impulses, the alternative runs thus: 'I should like to eat that, or I should like to spit it out.'" In normal grief, the oral impulses, which in melancholia savagely attack the introjected object, are modified, tamed, and sublimated, and they turn against this object and the ego in the process of judging them. Like judgment, epistemophilia—the craving to know—is a modified expression of oral wishes. This impulse, too, comes into play in the reality testing that is the nuclear process of the grief work, and it is gratified in the grief study of the object and the grieving ego. It is probable that because of this impulse many persons enter analysis shortly after losing a love object, needing that facilitation of the work of mourning which comes with analytic working through, and turning their self-judging and self-curiosity into analytic self-study.

Mourning has its limitations as a method of attaining insight and a cure. It cannot get at unconscious representations and affects under all circumstances, as Freud showed in melancholia. It cannot always make the intellectual insight into the object relationship sufficiently efficacious, and denial and other defenses may get the upper hand. Sadness, like elation, acts as a resistance to the appreciation of other buried affects and may be used to exclude or preclude them. However, as Abraham noted (1924), normal mourning may terminate in a heightened sense of well-being, increased sexual potency and capacity for work, and sublimation. These are not, I think, as Abraham interpreted them, normal analogues of mania, but the "good analytic result" of the work of mourning.

CHAPTER VIII

ACCORDING to psychoanalysis, the people who develop psychogenic illness are those who, in the face of the emotional conflicts produced in childhood by disappointment, have reacted to their real helplessness by a denial of the disappointment and the assertion of their omnipotent power to satisfy their pleasure-seeking and destructive instincts. This flight from reality takes the form of fantasies of terrific mutilations (the so-called castration complex) which arouse in them a mixture of triumph, terror, rage, remorse and sexual feeling, bringing with them the fear of monstrous retributions which may be too terrifying to be faced and so are repressed. In extreme cases *no* outlet for the pleasure-seeking instinct escapes this taint of sexualised cruelty so that none can be indulged with an easy mind. *Any* satisfaction of theirs now unconsciously appears to them to mean the destruction and ruin of all concerned, their own aggression destroying that which they desire and involving themselves in the disaster as a just retribution. When Oscar Wilde wrote "For each man kills the thing he loves", I suppose he was talking about his own ambivalence. A patient burst into tears and said, "Whenever I touch anything beautiful, I have to spoil it".

Because of this entanglement with destructive impulses, pleasure-seeking has to be repressed, and so sexual development is arrested at an immature and primitive level. Anxiety tends to appear whenever the barrier of repression weakens or when pressure from the repressed impulses is increased. It is a question of the equilibrium between two opposing forces. If the pressure from the unconscious threatens to outweigh the repressing forces, the only alternatives are either to give up the claim to omnipotence, which means admitting the reality of the early failure, but at the same time being released from the anxiety and guilt which this claim to omnipotence brings with it, or else to keep the omnipotent guilty fantasies, by means of which the failure was denied, and find some *modus vivendi* with them which shall allow them to disturb consciousness as little as possible. The first of these ways of dealing with the problem is the only one which can rightly be regarded as completely healthy. No one can be considered in perfect mental health while he cherishes repressed delusions and needs to defend himself against fantasies of omnipotence which threaten to erupt, and so constitute a potential source of anxiety and guilt having no foundation in external reality.

Complete contact with reality, however, is a counsel of perfection which mankind has certainly not yet attained: everyone does cherish unconscious delusions and is therefore not ideally sane. The degree of mental health depends on the proportion of the total energy which is being used up in repressed fantasy, and in the effort needed to keep it out of consciousness. It might even perhaps be measurable, at least theoretically, in terms of the amount of anxiety and guilt, conscious or unconscious, against which defence is needed. Even when a great deal of energy is being wasted in the repression of omnipotent delusions, it does not follow that the person will be obviously neurotic. Granted that the presence of repressed sexualised hostility is causing considerable unconscious anxiety and guilt, this only means that there is a need to find ways of preventing what has been repressed from upsetting the rest of the personality which has maintained contact and adapted itself to reality.

One way of meeting the difficulty is by the creation of *psychogenic symptoms*. This defence has already been discussed. The alternative defences against interference from what has been repressed are *more repression*, further reinforced perhaps by a protective scheme of life, or else the easing of tension by *sublimation*.

Among all those people who would ordinarily be counted as normal, or even as remarkably well balanced, I believe a surprisingly large number are making use of the whole scheme of their existence as an unremitting defence against unconscious anxiety and guilt. This defence is often so successful that no suspicion of uneasiness reaches clear consciousness, and yet their whole career may really have been unconsciously inspired, and still be dominated, by the need to neutralise anxiety. These

The Wish to Fall Ill

lives differ from real normality and health in the restless drive which seems to force them on. Such people cannot enjoy relaxation. Here it is not a matter of giving an outlet to repressed fantasies by any particular substituted activity, as occurs in symptoms or sublimations: the whole of their lives seems to be a grand organised phobia, designed to avoid finding themselves in some type of situation which to them is intolerable. For some, the intolerable situation might be helplessness, and it might thus be necessary for them at all costs to avoid being in any situation which they could not control. For others, the danger situation might be envy or jealousy, and life has to be arranged to avoid the possibility of ever coming into conflict with a successful rival. For others, what cannot be tolerated is disappointment; they must not ask and fail to receive. Others must never meet with contradiction and risk having their temper roused. Others, on account of their unconscious guilt, must spend their lives making restitution.

All these anxiety situations have much in common and could be related back to the emotional conflict provoked by the original disappointment of early pleasure-seeking, that is, either to dread of being left in a state of unsatisfied desire, or else to castration or mutilation anxiety.

They may be avoided in two opposite ways. Failure may be ensured against, either by limiting the demands made on life, withdrawing from the struggle and avoiding competition, taking no risks; or else by making demands, but seeing to it that they are always satisfied. In the case of those who take no risks, the limitation of their ambitions may perhaps suggest something amiss, though for the most part they pass as ordinary inconspicuous people; but those whose lives are pathologically organised round success are usually regarded as patterns of health. They may make use of all the normal outlets and appear to lead full and satisfying lives.

An analyst reported a case[1] of this sort who would be held up as a pattern of normal womanhood. She devoted her life to home pursuits, childbirth, and the education of her children, and

[1] Case of Miss Ella F. Sharpe reported in *The International Journal of Psychoanalysis*, vol. XII, "The Technique of Psychoanalysis".

Defence Mechanisms: Treatment

seemed a conspicuously well-adapted wife and mother. Nevertheless, her feminine activities were all compulsive. They were not followed simply for their own sake, but were as necessary to her in defending herself against the anxiety connected with her deep rivalry with other women as a phobia is to a frank neurotic. If she could not produce babies, she fell into anxiety as severe as the anxiety of a claustrophobic patient who is forced to go into the Underground, or is shut up in a cupboard.

Throughout their lives such people are dominated, just as the neurotic is, by the need for security against anxiety, but, whereas in symptom-formation the patient's energy is dissipated in symbolic performances which have little or no real use, this other type of defence is often played out in terms of real achievements. It falls short of true mental health because, however real the achievements may be, they are inspired, not so much by reality considerations, as by the delusion of dangers which do not in fact exist. The driving force is not healthy pleasure, but fear.

I feel sure that the analysis of a great many personalities who have achieved the most brilliant successes would bring to light some such state of affairs. Their achievements would be found to rest, not so much on the happy realisation of their instincts, as on inner compulsion; they do not merely enjoy what they do and so do it well, they *must* succeed on penalty of falling into acute morbid anxiety, and any check which threatens their defensive scheme of life throws them into a fury or panic. Many brilliant students and prominent men of affairs belong to this class. Some of them carry on successfully right through life— every now and then one breaks down from what is called "over-work", and then the inner strain of their terrific achievement becomes apparent. Such people cannot really be regarded as in perfect mental health, even if no breakdown ever comes to betray them, but they belong, obviously, to a different class from the neurotics or the insane. Indeed they constitute an important section of the population which, in our civilisation, is regarded as entirely, and even typically, normal.

The other "normal" way of dealing with unconscious anxiety and guilt is by *sublimation*. Sublimation consists in the trans-

The Wish to Fall Ill

ferring of the value with which the pleasure-seeking instinct normally endows the objects of its desire on to other objects not in themselves sexual. Simple sublimation would result if the instinct transferred was nothing but pleasure-seeking or love, and such sublimation would no doubt play an important part in complete mental health. But while unconscious anxiety and guilt persist sublimation is necessarily more complicated, since, besides being carried on for its own sake, it has also to be used defensively. Used in this way, however, it is far more practically successful than the other alternatives of symptom-formation and repression. Both allow a partial outlet for repressed impulses, but whereas the symptom, though it may compensate by denial and punishment for the forbidden gratification, yet always manages somehow to include an element of destruction and revenge which perpetuates the guilt and demands always more and more repression, sublimation, while it also gives expression to repressed ambivalent impulses, yet neutralises the guilt which gratification arouses by perpetually making restitution in symbolic form for the destructive wishes. Surgery may be an obvious example of such sublimation, in which cutting up the body combines injury and cure, and the giving of anaesthetics is another illustration, since here the patient is overpowered and reduced to a condition resembling death itself, but yet this is done to spare him and is indeed an act of mercy.

The lives of many people are, I think, built up on this plan. From their dreams and all their creative work it is clear that they must still have in them somewhere the same sort of unconscious preoccupations as also find expression in neurotic symptoms and insanity.

The analysis of all those socially permitted activities, such as art, literature, philanthropy, music, cooking, cleaning, typewriting, agriculture, learning, science, research, teaching, singing, business, finance, and so on (that is, any of the vocations that a healthy person may take up), strongly suggests that they are often transformations of our early primitive preoccupations no less than symptoms are. Furthermore, they would often appear to be used as acts of restitution designed continually to allay the guilt which torments those who unconsciously cherish

Defence Mechanisms: Treatment

great hostility, and unconsciously believe that their destructive fantasies have succeeded[1].

One case in point was a woman of thirty, who had been determined from childhood to become a painter and had succeeded, against a good deal of opposition, in getting her parents to allow her to give up her other education and go to an art school when she was fifteen. She seems to have shown considerable talent, but she became discouraged after a year and spent the next fifteen years of her life taking up one thing after another and then dropping it.

After a few months' analysis, she came to the decision, which she had always been secretly hoping to make, but had always put off, to return to her painting. She liked especially to draw women, but complained of the *flatness* of her work. She could not get the contours *rounded*. She was evidently ambivalent about women's bodies, and in her drawing alternated between bad days when the figures seemed to be squashed out flat, and good days when they were full. At a later period she was worried for a time by an exaggeration of roundness in which she complained that her paintings looked as if they were "blown out and too full".

In this outlet of art she seemed to be working out a mixture of impulses, some destroying, some restoring and recreating the bodies which she drew. The unconscious struggle between flatness and roundness turned on the subject of pregnancy.

I made some interpretations to this effect, which roused feelings of guilt and alarmed her. She found it difficult to follow what I said, appearing not to have understood, and she told me plainly, in her next association, though without realising consciously that she was doing it, to leave her alone and not to make her aware of what she meant unconsciously by her painting, and then she said, defensively, and with embarrassment, "Do you know what I really want to paint is a picture of Mother Earth, which shall represent her as quite perfect".

During a period of less repressed hostility to women's bodies she took to chopping pieces of wood and felt that she would like

[1] See also an article in the *International Journal of Psychoanalysis*, by Ella F. Sharpe, vol. XI, part 1, Jan. 1930, "Certain Aspects of Sublimation and Delusion".

to change over to carving or stone-cutting, thus unconsciously attempting to utilise her aggressive impulses in the interests of creation.

Prior to her return to painting she had been turning her hostility back on herself, sometimes in the form of masturbation with fantasies of torture, sometimes in the form of acute self-depreciation which even led her to threaten suicide.

As she gained further insight into the ambivalent conflict which disturbed her painting, and which had formerly driven her to abandon it, an improvement appeared in her work, the incentive to paint shifting over, from the need to make restitution, towards creation, inspired by more unmixed love and pleasure. This is only a single case and comparatively simple. I agree that we have no right to generalise from it to theories about the unconscious meaning of art, or still less of sublimations in general. But analysts are all the time collecting material about this subject, and it appears to point in the direction which I have indicated. namely, that both psychogenic symptoms and sublimations give indirect expression to the pleasure-seeking instinct which has become repressed because of its entanglement with destructive impulses: but that, whereas in symptoms the destructive impulses appear, deflected but essentially unchanged, in the useless form of self-inflicted pain, in sublimation of this defensive kind the destructive impulses are turned to advantage, in that the very activities whereby the destruction is symbolically achieved—as for instance, the cutting or soiling of the material in sculpture or painting—are used to make symbolic restitution—as in creating a statue or picture—thus making the sublimated activity acceptable in a way that the mere symptom could never be. Even the destructive component is now made use of, whereas with symptoms it is destructive only, and so has to be atoned for by pain.

Symptoms thus fail to meet the problem of anxiety and guilt, while sublimation solves it. It remains true, however, that so long as the delusion persists of the magical power of destructive fantasy and the supposed retribution which it will bring, such repressed fantasies remain as a constant menace which must always be met by some measure of defence.

Defence Mechanisms: Treatment

The ideal solution would be to get rid of the delusions and gain contact with reality.

Even in perfect mental health the hostile and destructive impulses which disappointment and jealousy arouse would still, to some extent, remain, but instead of being endowed with all sorts of monstrous omnipotent destructive powers and expected to provoke murderous retributions, the everyday acts in which they find daily expression with all of us would be recognised as the attenuated and comparatively harmless pieces of cruelty or spite which in fact they are, and so would no longer give rise to morbid anxiety and guilt. And, indeed, when the unconscious reasons for the delusional fears from which so much of our hostility actually springs became conscious and were seen to be unfounded, much of the cruelty and spite would disappear automatically.

The absence of these delusions and of the morbid anxiety and guilt which follows in their train might be taken as the criterion of perfect normality. Such a normal person, having really outgrown the delusions produced at the time of his early struggles, would be able to see situations as they are and react to them in a way that was really appropriate. Real dangers would, I suppose, arouse fear and efforts to protect himself, even in the ideally normal person, but he would not be constantly imagining danger when it was not there, nor seeking self-destruction. He would not be afraid to experience living, and he would escape the neurotic guilt which comes from the persisting unconscious infantile belief in the omnipotence of his own hostile impulses, and the chastisement which the archaic conscience inflicts upon most of us on this account.

Possibly it may be felt that such a person would be inhuman. I have heard people express alarm that analysis might too successfully relieve people of their endearing weaknesses. But fantastic anxiety and guilt are not endearing weaknesses! There would be no danger of dullness or tediousness resulting from being relieved of such a bugbear, and I wish it might be possible to be entirely rid of it. Actually, however, analysis can hardly hope to do more than relieve the patient of the excessive burden which he carries over from the past as compared with that of

39

the average man, so that he need not check himself at every turn, but can at least dare to permit himself a glimpse of things as they really are, divested of fantastic terrors.

For, as it is, the neurotic hardly comes in contact with reality at all. Because of his excessive unconscious dread of renewed disappointment and the conflicting passions into which he fears this would again plunge him, he has never given himself the opportunity to grow beyond the primitive outlook of his unconscious, which still dominates his adult relations with the outside world, as it did in infancy with all of us. The fundamental thing about the neurotic outlook is that essentially it has remained primitive. It is still profoundly ambivalent, still believes in its own omnipotence, still projects its own impulses and its own omnipotence on the outside world.

Thus, it is clear that there is a great deal in the neurotic's deepest attitude towards life which has simply never grown up at all, however adult and intellectual and cultivated he may seem in ordinary social encounters. We all, it is true, in our customary relations with people tend to put up some amount of bluff, though perhaps our bluff succeeds better in disguising us from ourselves than from them. This is much truer of the neurotic, and the more severe his illness the more true it becomes. The neurotic's conscious social personality is necessarily always a kind of bluff: what really governs his life is something quite different, something quite unconscious, because deeply repressed; and, however civilised and philosophic and tolerant the surface personality may be, this repressed unconscious is invariably primitive.

It is this repressed primitive part which is responsible for psychogenic illness and speaks through the symptoms, dreams, fantasies and free-associations of patients, and obviously these expressions of the unconscious will not be properly intelligible until we have some idea of how unconscious mental processes work and how they differ from the normal adult thinking with which we are familiar. I believe it is possible to formulate a few essential characteristics which distinguish primitive mental processes from the thinking of more adult type. They depend on the relation to reality.

Defence Mechanisms: Treatment

The first and perhaps the most striking characteristic of primitive thinking is that it is *not hampered by any need for consistency*. While disbelieving and denying, it can also, in the same breath, believe, or it can believe contradictory things simultaneously. Logicians of the unconscious might call this the first law of unconscious thought, but it is the exact opposite of the first law of thought in conscious logical mental operations.

The second distinguishing characteristic of primitive thinking is the belief in the *omnipotence of thoughts and wishes*.

The third is the *confusion of fact with fantasy, thinking with doing*.

The fourth is the *small importance attached to knowing and the all-importance of wishing*.

The fifth is the *complete failure to distinguish from one another things which are somehow emotionally identified*.

The mental operations of the unconscious seem to be primitive in all these senses. With regard to the first point—its disregard of consistency—the neurotic's ambivalent attitude is a striking example of this type of self-contradiction, and again and again in dreams, symptoms and fantasies we find that contradictory wishes and contradictory attitudes and beliefs are being expressed simultaneously by the same symbol or action without the contradiction being felt as any difficulty.

As regards the second point—the feeling of omnipotence—the unconscious fails to recognise the limitations of its own powers. This primitive belief in the omnipotence of thought is what makes the child's megalomania, his belief in magic, his fantastic image of the parents which, failing to distinguish between the self and the outside world, he constructs on the pattern of what he believes himself to be. This omnipotent attitude characterises the savage, the madman and the dreamer, and it persists unconsciously in the neurotic too. The advantages from the point of view of pride and the denial of disappointment and helplessness are obvious, and on account of these advantages the belief in omnipotence is hard to give up. To give it up is to admit the danger and humiliation of powerlessness and is felt as reopening the door to all the intolerable pain and anxiety which once belonged to the psychophysical helplessness of unsatisfied infantile needs.

The Wish to Fall Ill

On the other hand, the belief in omnipotence brings with it its own terrors and anxieties. For the primitive mind believes in the omnipotence of *all* its wishes, including the revengeful, destructive ones. The savage works magic to make rain, to make the crops grow, to bring success; but also he works magic to destroy, and he believes in this black magic quite as much as, or more than, the other, and so lives always in dread of black magic turning back against himself. In the neurotic this sense of his omnipotence leads to feelings of guilt and terror, as well as to excessive self-glorification, both inflated in proportion to the persisting strength of the delusion of omnipotence.

The third characteristic of primitive thinking is the failure to distinguish fact from fantasy, thinking from doing. It, too, brings with it its own special advantages and dangers. At the most primitive level of all, this failure is complete when fancy reaches the vividness of actual hallucination. The madman, reverting to his early attitude, withdraws his interest from reality and substitutes his own delusions. In doing so he escapes the disappointments of real life. But, since the wish is not distinguished from the deed, mere fantasies of destruction are enough to arouse all the guilt and terror, which, at the adult level, could only be justified by the doing of real damage.

In dreams, delirium or fantasy reality is similarly forgotten and we are taken up with the productions of our own unconscious. Sometimes these are pleasant compensations for reality disappointment, but here, once again, panic may come out in nightmares. This withdrawing from contact with reality marks a regression to an earlier kind of mental process which is preoccupied exclusively with wishing and has no interest in true perception.

The most primitive level of the mind would seem to be entirely taken up with pleasure-seeking, and if what it seeks is not forthcoming in reality, it supplies the deficiency by imagination or even hallucination. The repressed unconscious of the neurotic appears to function at this level and we can never understand its creations, such as dreams, fantasies, hallucinations, delusions, psychogenic symptoms and sublimations unless we remember that the driving forces behind them, no matter how self-contradictory or painful or senseless they may appear to be, *are always ultimately wishes*. Usually what is wanted is so unfamiliar or actually unwelcome to adult thinking, and so disguised and over-determined and condensed, and often contains such a large element of pain and punishment, that the wish-fulfilment is by no means obvious. But occasionally in dreams the simple wish-fulfilment is clear and no conflict disturbs the satisfaction.

Otto Nodenskjold in his book *Antarctic* (1904) tells of the experiences of the crew who passed the winter with him. He says they all dreamed vividly. "Eating and drinking formed the central point around which most of our dreams were grouped. One reported in the morning that he had had a dinner consisting of three courses. Another dreamt of tobacco, whole mountains of tobacco."

Freud quotes the dream of a friend while he was a medical student. This young man had been vigorously called by his landlady but was most unwilling to get up. Instead of waking and going to hospital he dreamt of a room in a hospital with a bed in which he was lying. A chart with his name and age was pinned over his head. Reassuring himself with the thought, "Since I am already in hospital, I need not go", he turned over and slept on.

The superficial wish-fulfilment in these dreams is obvious. To interpret them fully no doubt one would need to go deeper and look for wishes more important and more repressed, whose fulfilment in the dream is correspondingly disguised. But the point I am concerned with in these illustrations is to remark that the dream fulfilment of such innocent wishes as here appear can be represented quite openly just because there is no harm in them. It is when pleasure-seeking and destructive impulses are aroused simultaneously that there comes in conflict, and with it the need for greater distortion.

The final essential characteristic of primitive thinking is the *failure to distinguish things which are emotionally similar*. The meaning of reality is all in terms of instinct satisfaction. Whatever arouses the same instincts *is* the same. To the baby all men are, to begin with, "Daddy", all furry things "pussy". If one original pussy frightened the baby, all the other pussy things frighten it and it does not attend to the difference between them.

Analysis and discrimination seem to be later achievements at a more adult level which the unconscious has never reached. Situations which have little unconscious significance may be nicely discriminated; but when anything really stirs a repressed emotion, the reaction to it is primitive—it is not distinguished from the earlier situations to which that emotion remains attached.

The emotions which the neurotic has repressed being essentially his love and his hate (or, more accurately, his sexualised hostility), anyone who later stirs this emotion is at once unconsciously assimilated to the earlier love-hate objects.

All men and women who become important to him, in his unconscious fantasy are simply father and mother over again. All aggression tends to have the unconscious significance of murder of rivals or of frustrating love-objects, all disappointment the significance of weaning, early discipline, or the first frustration of love. The Oedipus situation, which has been described in the preceding two chapters, is confused with all later important relationships so that these are reacted to, not on their own merits, but as if they still were this first one, thus unconsciously re-animating the old omnipotent fantasies and the old mutilation terrors.

It follows that he will repeat the same failures over and over again, because, in his unconscious, which governs his life, he fails to recognise that there is any alteration. The unconscious is still in the nursery; it is fixated there.

But there is an important reason for this fixation and the repetition which it brings about, and this is that with all their pains and frustrations and disappointments, these early nursery emotional experiences remain for these people the type of sexual satisfaction, and they fly towards them again and again, inevitably, like a moth to a candle, always getting stunned and scorched, but perpetually returning to renew the attempt. Such perseverance of instinct striving which still goes on and on inevitably seeking its object, learning nothing by its failures and never daunted, is more like the blind persistence of insects than the intelligent adaptations which characterise human beings;

Defence Mechanisms: Treatment

and indeed in this matter the neurotic, as long as his repression holds absolute, is reduced to the inevitable and hopeless instinctiveness of creatures much lower than himself in the evolutionary scale. No matter what the cost, he seeks the old Oedipus situation of frustration, which for him means sexuality, seeing nothing in any new situation of life, but still always the same old figures of father, mother, brothers and sisters, or rather, not even these, but only their Imagos, wildly distorted by the projections of childish fantasy.

Thus to the extent that anyone is actuated by repressed unconscious drives he behaves like a mechanism rather than like a living creature. He is utterly determined and can do nothing but fatally repeat one reaction. It is only in so far as he escapes repression, or is later able to lift it, that he chooses freely in the only sense in which freedom seems to have any meaning, that is, he makes his choice with his whole self, recognising his present situation and using his past experience to secure the most complete satisfaction of which reality admits.

Having now completed my statement of the psychoanalytic theory concerning the origin and meaning of psychogenic illness, I cannot end without saying something more about its treatment, though what I say on this subject must be brief.

I have explained that the neurotic, dominated by his earlier emotional attitudes, which were repressed during his "Oedipus" struggles, will endow everybody with whom he comes in contact with the attributes of the Parent Imagos either consciously or unconsciously. Schoolmasters, employers, officials, will all be reacted to as if they were the original parental figures as they then appeared to the small child. A 'bus driver who will not stop when he is hailed may call up a passion of fury: a policeman may evoke terrible feelings of guilty dread.

It is an essential characteristic of neurosis to make such emotional confusions or, as ey are technically call " transferences ", l the time , on to everyone, and it is to be expected that this will still happen when treatment is attempted. The patient who has already made transferences to the policeman and the 'bus driver will now make one to his doctor. If he has

15-2

45

defied or cringed before his father and later before schoolmasters or employers, he may do the same before his analyst.

It would be foolish, of course, to say that the neurotic is incapable of any appreciation of reality: this may be true in extreme cases of insanity, but the neurotic is only partly deluded, and is mainly in contact with the outside world. Nevertheless, it is true that the neurotic patient shows considerable lack of reality sense in human relations when his fantasies are allowed to develop unchecked, as happens in the analytic situation. The analyst is loved, feared or hated for quite other than reality reasons.

What made the patient ill originally was not his love but his hostile emotions, and it is these which still stand in the way of cure. Because of them he mistrusts himself and everyone with whom he comes in contact. This mistrust, which runs through his whole life, naturally appears also in the analytical situation. Here too, as elsewhere, the patient will manifest his terror of human contact which springs from his repressed mutilation fantasies. When the delusions on which this terror rests are understood and seen through as they reappear in relation to the analyst, the barriers between the patient and the rest of the world are also removed and he can make what contacts he pleases. The neurotic mistrust of human contacts rests on the repressed mutilation fantasies of mutual injury by devouring, strangling, burning, cutting or whatever it may be. It is these which interfere with reality contact and cause the patient to make stereotyped transference reactions of aggression or fear.

The successful outcome of a Freudian psychoanalysis consists in the patient being released from the need to make transference reactions and enabled instead to react to present-day reality.

It might be supposed that a patient would welcome the attempt to discover these fantasies in order to dispel them and that he would relinquish them gladly, but this is by no means the case. On the contrary, he clings to them because, unconsciously, they still represent the fulfilment of his sexual and hostile impulses, and he *wants* them to be true. At the same time, he is terrified of them, and puts up every conceivable defence

Defence Mechanisms: Treatment

against becoming aware of them, and this, for the same reason as he originally fell ill and still remains so, namely that the repression of these fantasies appears to him to be the only possible way of escaping mortal danger and intolerable pain. His life has been spent in fighting the danger of becoming aware of them, and the fight continues throughout the analysis. At every turn he holds himself in check lest, in becoming aware of what he unconsciously dreams of doing, he should be impelled to carry it out in actual fact.

The analysis progresses to the extent to which the patient gains insight into these repressed fantasies. But encouraging him to dare to relax his repression and risk becoming aware of what, unconsciously, he still wants, is, of course, not the same thing as inviting him to *carry out* the primitive urges against which he has all his life been struggling. He advances in his cure essentially by knowing what he wants to do, whether he does it or not. Mere acting out of his wishes blindly would not be of the slightest use. But in so far as his unconscious cannot distinguish between thinking a thing and doing it, he is bound to fight against the analysis, regarding it as a direct incentive to the actions he most abhors, because they are actually his strongest temptations. There are certainly times when the analyst, around whom his unconscious fantasies have entwined themselves, must appear in the disguise of the Arch Tempter.

Transference is not a new phenomenon created by analysis: and it did not occur for the first time in this relationship; it intrudes continually into the patient's daily life also and colours his relations with everyone. He has his own ways, in ordinary relationships of dealing with the situations which these fantasies produce, and he will use them again in analysis. If he fears disappointment and the fury which this rouses in himself so that he dare not enter into any close contacts, he will mistrust the analytic relationship also, hold his body stiffly, speak softly, and keep the doctor at arm's length. If he is dominated by unconscious starvation so that he needs in all relationships to get as much as possible, he will try to *get* things once more in this new situation, demanding explanations perhaps or being hungrily determined to get his utmost out of every hour. If he

The Wish to Fall Ill

resented being made to part with his faeces he may refuse to give his free-associations and upbraid the doctor for charging any fees.

All these characteristic ways of behaving to present situations under the influence of past conflicts or repressed fantasies are instances of transference.

In ordinary life he may manage to get a fair semblance of outside justification for the fears, resentments, remorses, suspicions, contempts or passionate devotions which he experiences, and there may of course be considerable reality grounds for all or at least for some of them. But in the analysis, reality contact is reduced to a minimum, and so here the part played by fantasy in what he feels and thinks stands out with especial clearness.

Under the influence of the fantasies which begin to emerge consciously in the analytic situation, the patient's idea of the analyst's character and probable reactions and even of his appearance will at times turn out to be surprisingly wide of the mark. A friend, who is exceptionally thin and fair, tells me that one of his patients, who had actually seen him daily for many months, believed him to be portentously fat and so dark that she thought he had negro blood. The patient's idea of the analyst's character is also continually altering in accordance with the fantasies which are uppermost. He may, for instance, transfer on to the analyst the same horror and condemnation which he really feels towards his own repressed sexual fantasies, or towards the monstrous Parent Imagos on whom those fantasies were modelled. Mr J., it will be remembered, thought of me as some sort of a vampire who was trying to drain his vitality and who might rob him of his penis. To him, at that time, I appeared depraved and dangerous. At other times the analyst, who is identified either with the patient's idea of his parents or of his own self, may appear ridiculous or contemptible, or, on the other hand, when love is transferred, he may appear angelic.

The patient's impulses towards the analyst also vary similarly in accordance with fantasy, and sometimes the pregenital nature of what is wanted is quite clear. One patient, warning me not to encourage her to express her real feelings, told me she would

Defence Mechanisms: Treatment

be too much for me if she let herself go, and would separate me from everyone else, feeling as if she would actually devour me. That night she had a nightmare in which she found herself in my house uninvited eating something she was not entitled to. At another time she felt as if she might strangle me.

The analyst's room becomes involved in the aggression which must originally have been directed towards the bodies of the people who figured in the early situations. Patients have had the impulse to burn up all my books or smash my furniture. The patient of whom I have just spoken expressed her jealousy of another whom she saw leaving my room by slapping the cushion on which the other's head had been lying. Another patient mentioned at the end of the hour that she had had a parallel train of thought going on all the time she was talking, which consisted in imaginarily chiselling off ornamental excrescences which decorated my mantelpiece. Her intentions towards me must have been hostile, for just before mentioning this she had remarked, "I can see that it is only because I am holding myself back that I haven't been downright abusive". I think the bits which were to be chiselled off my mantelpiece represented deeper fantasies of chiselling bits off me.

In the course of this acting-out of earlier repressed situations, the transference is continually shifting so that the analyst stands now for one of the original figures, now for another, and for these figures in different aspects, sometimes loved, sometimes hated, or again he may stand for different aspects of the patient's own self.

The close identification of the patient himself with the other figures, love- or hate-objects or rivals, who were involved in the early emotional conflicts, is very striking. His love, hate and blame are continually being shifted, now inwards, now outwards, and in all the various parts played out the analyst has his share. It is just this re-enacting of the old drama that gives the opportunity for new and valuable insight, and it can thus be seen how very important it is that the analyst should be detached enough to recognise the repetition meaning of all the various attitudes that are from time to time attributed to him or felt about him.

The Wish to Fall Ill

I am not denying of course that the patient and analyst have some real relation to each other also, but it is essential for the progress of the treatment to distinguish what is real from what is transferred and based actually, not on present reality, but on the confusion of this with repressed fantasies carried over from the past.

To the unconscious of the patient the new situations appear naturally as opportunities for gratification, in so far as the old impulses which are now re-animated seem to hold out a promise of pleasure. On the other hand, in so far as the new situations revive old mutilation fantasies, bringing with these old terrors, there may be from time to time accesses of panic. The analysis now appears to the patient's unconscious not as an opportunity for gratification but as a danger terrifying in proportion to the terrors of the fantasies which are being re-lived again in connection with the figure of the analyst. At such times fear of the treatment may severely tax the patient's determination to persevere with the cure. At one time Mr J. did in fact break off treatment for three months in an access of castration terror. Another patient, whose castration fear was also very severe, jumped up and left the room twice in a sudden outburst of rage which masked his terror, but, summoning up his courage and dimly recognising the fantasy nature of his fears, came back within a few minutes and resumed his analysis.

It is the analyst's business to keep firm hold of the transferred significances of the patient's various attitudes towards the treatment, and, in spite of appeals, threats, or panics, to keep steadily to the single object of using this transference situation to bring to light the unconscious fantasies upon which all the patient's transference reactions rest, that is, the unconscious sources of his illness, so that he may at last be convinced that the need to react in this way has no objective justification, but springs from an internal compulsion, based ultimately on the delusion of his own omnipotent dangerousness and the corresponding dangerousness of other people.

Progressively with the renunciation of this delusional belief anxiety and guilt subside, and he becomes able to tolerate erotic and hostile impulses in himself, as these occur, without immediately dissociating them in a panic, as he has been accustomed to do all his life. Gradually, as he tests reality, as he finds it in the analytical situation, it begins to dawn upon him that his fantastic terrors are groundless. He hates the analyst, and nothing happens, the analyst neither dies nor turns upon him and destroys him. He loves the analyst, and again nothing happens—no avenging rival appears, neither does love burn him up. Slowly he begins to be able to allow his attention to rest upon his own real situation, and so at last he gives himself a chance to know it.

It is this change in the lifelong panic reaction to reality which is aimed at. When that is accomplished, real satisfaction and pure sublimation become possible, and the symptoms cease to be necessary.

Thus in Freudian analysis the transference of the repressed infantile beliefs, wishes and terrors, which the patient has in fact always been making throughout life, and which constitute his illness, is recognised and accepted by the doctor as it occurs once again in relation to the analysis, and is used to cure the patient by enabling him, in the midst of re-living it once more in the consulting room, at last to see through it and finally free himself from it.

Before Freud, the whole question of transference in neurosis had never been given due weight: it was Freud who first recognised transference, not as a mere symptom occasionally occurring perhaps in certain types of hysteria, but as universal and inevitable in all neurosis. And it was Freud who devised the method of analysis by which the transference can be used to get rid of itself.

Unfortunately, there are still many psychotherapists who fail to recognise how inevitable transference is in neurotic patients, and how great a part it plays in all their relationships with the outside world, and, in failing to see this they necessarily also fail to realise the valuable use to which transference may be put in the treatment of psychogenic illness. Some doctors, while they admit reluctantly that transference does occur in some cases, regard it as regrettable, and pride themselves that with their *own* patients at any rate they do not let it arise.

The Wish to Fall Ill

On the Freudian hypothesis concerning the neurotic's unconscious distortion of all his later relations in the light of his unconscious preoccupations, this can only mean that, failing to recognise it, they do not allow the open development of the transference to take place, which can only mean that it remains unexpressed; it cannot help being there, since, so long as the neurotic clings to the unconscious delusions which underlie his repressed mutilation fantasies, he is bound to misinterpret reality, and this misrepresentation *is* transference.

The fantastic fears which, according to our hypothesis, underlie transference form the basis on which much of what passes for normal life really rests. We have seen that they may be the driving force in primitive conscience. These fears may give rise to a submissiveness which can be, and often is, utilised to enforce obedience and conformity. This same submissiveness and infantile docility to authority has long been used consciously and unconsciously in medicine. Many forms of therapy depend on it and by means of it it is sometimes possible to induce patients to give up their symptoms. Hypnotism and suggestion probably work, in so far as they do work, by taking advantage of this transference attitude. But while the cure depends upon this infantile docility, based ultimately upon fear and delusion, it cannot dispel these and thus cannot free the patient of his neurosis: it may modify symptoms, but it leaves the underlying cause untouched. It may alleviate the patient's condition in some respects, but there is a danger, as I have pointed out, that, in losing the symptom outlet, by the help of which anxiety and guilt were kept at bay, the patient may only suffer more severely. The mere removal of symptoms, while the underlying mutilation fantasies remain, will do nothing to alleviate the anxiety and guilt, and hence it happens that patients who have been cured in this way may later develop anxiety attacks or else protect themselves from these by a fresh outbreak of symptoms. Sometimes the result may be both anxiety and new symptom-formation, leaving the patient considerably worse off than before.

An interesting example of this occurred in the case of a woman who had suffered from heart attacks ever since her father's

Defence Mechanisms: Treatment

death from heart disease. Although she was to some extent invalided, she had led a fairly normal life until she was induced to see a specialist about her heart. After a thorough examination he decided that the disturbance of the heart's function was psychogenic; that organically the heart was healthy, and he succeeded in persuading the patient that this was the case. The heart attacks disappeared, but in place of them the patient developed severe anxiety, while a tendency to agoraphobia, which had occasionally worried her, now became so much increased that she was absolutely incapable of leaving her house and remained shut up in it for years without once venturing out.

It is the possibility of such unwelcome results as this that make one cautious about using transference merely to deprive the patient of his symptoms, without doing anything to dispel the mutilation fantasies out of which the symptoms arise.

The way in which the transference is used in psychoanalysis is not open to these objections. The cure of symptoms is here not the primary consideration, but rather the cure of the condition which makes symptoms necessary, the removal of the anxiety and guilt and the mutilation fantasies which caused them and against which the symptoms have been erected as defences, since it is these which are making the patient ill.

In all circumstances transference consists in reacting to present situations and people as if these repressed fantasies applied to them, as if the attacks and revenges with which these fantasies deal were really about to occur in connection with them. Transference to the analyst is used in psychoanalytic treatment to bring these repressed fantasies to light in the actual situation of the treatment on which they now become focused, so that, by simultaneously experiencing what all the anxiety and guilt were about, and at the same time recognising how little they now apply, the patient may rid himself of them.

It is thus clear what an ambitious attempt psychoanalysis is—the attempt to undo the unconscious delusions and unnecessary safeguards of a lifetime, the attempt to set the patient free to grow up. When people are apt to blame it for taking so long, and for its failures, perhaps they do not understand how colossal is the task it attempts.

The Wish to Fall Ill

Certainly, it is a serious undertaking which should not be entered upon by anyone not qualified to handle it, since it involves dealing with highly explosive material. It is not possible to avoid arousing anxiety at times during the bringing to light of alarming fantasies before the relief afforded by recognising their delusional nature has been obtained. From time to time the patient, in the throes of his struggle with the anxiety which may have been thus aroused, will produce temporary exacerbations of old symptoms or a variety of new ones, which would alarm a doctor who did not fully understand what he was attempting to do for the patient and which he might not know how to interpret.

When, for instance, unconscious mouth fantasies are stirring, the patient may become ravenous, or defend himself by refusing all food, or vomiting. When the fantasy is connected with the stolen faeces-penis-baby inside the body, accompanied by the fear of being robbed of this, there may be complete constipation: rage may be expressed in terms of flatulence giving severe abdominal pain. At times the patient may experience open anxiety, but sometimes he has no conscious awareness of the emotion, producing instead some of its psychological bodily expressions such as palpitation, cold sweats, giddiness, nausea, diarrhoea, trembling. The correct handling of all these transitory symptoms depends upon an ability to recognise the underlying unconscious fantasies in each case, so that by bringing these to consciousness the need for defence by symptoms may be removed and the anxiety concerning them dispelled by recognition of their unreality.

Merely to stir up such fantasies without helping the patient to see through them is to inflict useless suffering and may even be dangerous. Finally, the correct handling of the transference, which is so fundamental in psychoanalytic treatment, can only be done by one who understands thoroughly all the ways in which it manifests itself and is himself sufficiently free from guilt and anxiety to accept calmly whatever extremes of primitive hate, fear, aggression or love the patient may direct upon him. While admitting the emotional reality of these attitudes for the patient, he must be able always to recognise clearly the elements of transference and fantasy in the analytical relationship, since it is one of his main tasks to enable the patient to discriminate between what is transference and fantasy and what is real, and thereby to free himself from the delusions which are the source of his illness.

Only one who has himself been thoroughly analysed is properly equipped to undertake such a task.

Psychoanalysis is a serious undertaking for patient and doctor alike, and should not be begun lightly but only when there is need, and a determination, once having begun, to carry it through to the end.

Nevertheless, there is no doubt that, when at last the repressed unconscious delusions of neurosis are seen through and discarded in favour of reality, the need for symptoms is gone, and the patient is healthy in a sense in which only very few are healthy even among those who have never thought of themselves as ill.

SUMMARY

In order to prevent anxiety and the feeling of guilt from developing, those who suffer from repressed omnipotent destructive fantasies need to make use of defences. In earlier chapters we considered the recognisably abnormal way of defence by symptom-formation and the more common defence by repression, and in this chapter I have spoken of what might by contrast be called the "normal" defence mechanisms *by character reaction and by sublimations.*

I have pointed out the advantages which these defences have over symptom-formation, but have added that the ideal solution would be to outgrow the repressed infantile fantasies and not to be in need of defences at all.

I went on to enumerate the essential characteristics which distinguish the primitive infantile outlook of the unconscious from adult thinking. I explained that the unconscious has a complete disregard for consistency, believes in the magical power of thoughts and wishes, is taken up entirely with wishing and not concerned about knowing, confuses fantasy with fact, thinking with doing, and makes the same reaction to all situations which resemble one another, emotionally failing to discriminate one from the other.

I have concluded with a short description of the way in which psychoanalysis uses the transference of the patient's unconscious fantasies on to the analytical relationship to enable him to free himself from his unconscious delusions and gain contact with the real world.

The Danger of Defense Mechanism

THE education of children is a complex problem and it may be viewed from many angles. Our particular point of view is the hygienic one, that is, we are confining our discussion to certain factors that may either help or hinder the child in his task of achieving healthy attitudes toward himself and the outside world. In practice such hygienic schooling consists in this, that the child is taught to meet his little difficulties in a sane way. When he has learned to do that, and has formed the habit of doing so, he is prepared to cope wholesomely with the more serious situations that adult life will present.

DIFFICULTIES — THE COMMON LOT OF MAN

It is a fact, which we should calmly face, that life involves a struggle for everyone. The nature of the conflict and its intensity vary with individuals, for the temperaments and abilities of people are different and so are the circumstances in which they live their lives. But difficulties of some kind or other must come to everyone. We have previously remarked that it is not the actual adversities he meets which determine a person's mental health, it is the way he reacts to them. That truth can bear repetition. The interpretations which a man puts upon his relations with others, his habitual manner of judging himself and his own efforts, are the factors that decide whether he will be mentally healthy or unhealthy.

While we have emphasized the necessity of laying the foundations of sound attitudes in the early years we do not mean that the training to healthy viewpoints should end with childhood. The acquisition of a sane outlook on life and its problems is the work of many years. The maintenance of such an outlook is the business of a lifetime. It is precisely because everyone must encounter obstacles and wrestle with opposition that children need practice in adapting themselves to difficulties. The child should have experience of success, so that he will be protected against the paralyzing feeling of inadequacy. It is equally important that he be given exercise in reacting to failure, for in his later life he is certain to meet with reverses and defeats, and so his mental health will be largely influenced by the way he responds to them. The child's correct training is achieved, not by removing all difficulties from his path, but by teaching him how to handle them.

THE ADVANTAGE OF STRUGGLES

There is a distinct value in conflicts. They may be utilized to stimulate effort, to act as a spur to attainment, to serve as motives of activity. Lack of opposition makes for a false sense of complacency, it deprives a man of the opportunity of learning his own limitations. The person whose desires are never obstructed is likely to be wanting in the initiative that is required for success in a competitive world. The successful accomplishment of a hard task engenders a feeling of self-reliance. Experience of resistance is a practical necessity for intellectual growth and for the expansion of personality. One of the best safeguards of mental health is a well-formed character, and character is formed not by evading difficulties, but by meeting them boldly and conquering them.

People enjoy a contest so long as they are successful in it; while they are masters of the situation they are put on their mettle by the hindrances they encounter in it. The trouble begins when their feeling of self-respect is wounded, when the ego is galled by the sting of defeat. It may be said that abnormal conduct, when it is not caused by some bodily condition, is a confession of failure. It is a sign that a person has not adjusted himself when his hopes, ideals, or ambitions have been thwarted or opposed.

It is the rarest individual who is successful in all his undertakings, while on the other hand there are not many who are utter and complete failures. For the vast majority, the issue in the conflict between personal desires and actual circumstances, is partial victory and partial defeat. It is here that adjustments must be made. That individual deserves to be considered well-balanced and normal who accepts his successes without arrogance and submits to his failures without undue dejection.

People develop various attitudes toward their difficulties as a result of their experiences with reverses. For purposes of convenience we may classify such emotional sets under three headings.

FACING REALITY SQUARELY

The first has been called the *aggressive attitude*. People of this type admit defeat, they even acknowledge that they are responsible for it, when they are. But instead of being disheartened by their lack of success they are energized by it. Their failures become stimulants to better and more intelligent effort. They profit by their mistakes, they study to see how they may prevent their recurrence. Hence, they exert themselves more strenuously and more successfully when they encounter new opposition. This is the wholesome attitude toward difficulties and the man who has it is mentally healthy. His aggressiveness may make him difficult to live with, for such a battling spirit sometimes robs its possessor of consideration for the feelings of others, but a person of this kind is not in much danger of a mental breakdown. Whether he wins or loses in his struggle, he has taken a definite stand. He is in touch with reality, he reacts to conditions of life as they actually are, and so long as he does that he is normal. His interests are turned from himself to the outside world. He is *extraverted* and hence he is spared the strains that result from excessive brooding.

This is the attitude that should be cultivated in children. They must be trained to a frank recognition of their failures. They must be encouraged to meet their problems squarely and honestly. When they suffer defeats, they must be animated against discouragement, and shown how they may avoid a similar failure in the future. The ordinary difficulties that confront the child, in his school or in his social relations, afford excellent opportunities for imparting such lessons.

LAYING DOWN ONE'S ARMS

Opposed to this healthy aggressive spirit is another which might be called the *shrinking attitude*. It is manifested by the individual who admits defeat, and confesses that it is due to his own fault, but who is crushed by his failures. He broods over his reverses until he becomes bitter. Because of his lack of success he grows convinced that he is powerless against the forces with which he comes into conflict. When he conceives this attitude, he makes but a feeble effort in his attempt to attain his ends. A vicious circle is established, his failures bring about despondence, and his dejection guarantees further failures. It is obvious that this state of mind is a serious menace to both happiness and efficiency. It breeds moodiness, anxiety, dissatisfaction, and diffidence; it may even lead to melancholia. Individuals who are too sensitive to their failures, tend to become introspective. They swell the ranks of the *introverts* of whom we hear so much today.[1]

Children must be protected against this disastrous attitude. They should be guarded against losing their self-confidence and against being overwhelmed by a sense of defeat. The child who is already manifesting signs of depression is in urgent need of attention. If it is found that his dejection is the result of his failure to cope with his difficulties, he must be helped to a saner outlook on life. Reasoning with him may produce some good results although, generally speaking, this is not an effective method of animating dejected children, especially when they are young. They need tangible experience of success, they must be shown by laboratory methods that they can actually and successfully cope with their problems. Conditions should be so arranged that they may get the taste of victory./At times it may be necessary to invent triumphs for a dis-

[1]An introvert is one whose attention and interest are abnormally turned in upon himself. He is not adjusted to conditions as they are. He is wrapped up in himself. He is given to dissecting his own actions and examining his own motives. He is likely to be unduly solicitous of what other people may say or think of him. Such a mental state is morbid, it may easily lead on to serious mental disturbances.

heartened child, since it is better for him to enjoy a counterfeit conquest than never to know success at all. Even a spurious victory may arouse a sense of accomplishment which will encourage a dispirited person to put forth the effort that will win him real successes.

COMPROMISING WITH REALITY

A third method of reacting to life's difficulties is less straightforward than either of the two we have been discussing. It consists in trying to shift the blame for one's defeats to someone else, or to circumstances beyond one's control. People of this class admit the failure, but they are unwilling to acknowledge that they are responsible for it. They resort to the expedient of *compromising.* They distort the actual situation. They are not fully in touch with reality, because they will not accept conditions as they actually exist. Few persons are ready to admit that they are intellectually incompetent, or lacking in character, or deficient in ability. Hence, when a man has made a mess of things he may try to protect himself from blame or from the reproach of culpable failure. Instead of acknowledging that his lack of accomplishment, or his imperfect achievements are due to his own inadequacy, to his own neglect, or to his own laziness, he seeks some excuse. He may contend for instance that he married too young, that he was handicapped by poor health, that he never had the chances which others enjoy, that jealousy of others put insuperable obstacles in his path.

THE DANGER OF SUBTERFUGE

When the practice of trying to explain away one's faults or failures becomes habitual, it makes for intellectual dishonesty. It is highly objectionable, too, from the viewpoint of mental health, for every compromise bristles with dangers and difficulties. One compromise leads to another until the situation becomes too complex to handle. The liar must tell new lies to protect himself from the consequences of his previous falsehoods. In the course of time the situation becomes so tangled that he becomes enmeshed in his own subterfuges. The man who reports an event truthfully needs only to remember the occurrence as he actually observed it, while he who distorts his recital must be mindful of his previous fabrications. When the person who practices compromises is conscious that the explanation of his deficiencies is fraudulent, he is disturbed by the fear that someone may penetrate his disguise. Even when he is not fully aware of his deceit, it subjects him to a nervous strain because his compromising is productive of new failures. It robs him of initiative and causes him to excuse himself from effort.

There are many different types of compromises but whatever form they may take they are all motivated by the same desire. They are attempts to safeguard one's reputation in the eyes of others and to protect one's own feeling of self-respect. They are expedients for defending the ego, or putting it more baldly, for preserving one's pride. Hence, they are called "defense reactions" or "defense mechanisms," frequently they are referred to as "escape mechanisms," because they are employed in order to flee from some trying situation.

THE EARLY APPEARANCE OF COMPROMISING

There is ample reason for believing that most defense reactions trace their origin to childhood. Usually they could have been avoided. When a child begins to resort to compromising he should be given immediate attention, for defense mechanisms may be corrected with comparative ease provided they are attacked early and intelligently. Adults should be able to recognize the first signs of compromise in the children under their charge. They should be alive to the fact that apparently trivial defense mechanisms may develop into queer types of behavior, indeed these reactions may even lead on to gross mental diseases. This conviction will stimulate an effort to train the child to a candid admission of his shortcomings.

It is the business of adults to protect the young from the contagion of bad example. Children are alert to perceive defense mechanisms in parents and teachers, and they are quick to copy them. Most of us, at some time or other, have used these reactions in order to gain some advantage or to escape some inconvenience. A little self-examination might reveal that we employ these shortsighted expedients more frequently than we imagine.

SHIFTING THE BLAME TO OTHERS

A favorite way of escaping punishment, or reproach, is by lodging complaints against outside causes. The blame for one's actions or failures is attributed to some animate or inanimate agent. The boy excuses his poor showing in school by maintaining that the teacher is unfair, or that the examination is unjust — he was asked precisely those few questions that he did not know, the many others which he could have answered perfectly were not proposed at all. Some people lay the blame for their physical or mental flaws at the door of heredity. No one is responsible for his own heredity and, hence, he cannot be held accountable for its effects. The weather, the ill will of others, unforeseen accidents, and a host of other causes, are appealed to in order to defend oneself against censure. A vogue for astrology prompts some individuals to attribute their good or evil fortunes to "their stars."

Many people are persuaded that they are dominated by outside hostile forces; they imagine that others are causing them to think vile thoughts, or to act violently; they argue that they are under the malign influence of hypnotism, the radio, or mental telepathy. Such people have clear-cut delusions of persecution, they are in reality demented. But many of them might have preserved their mental integrity if they had been treated correctly, and in time.

It would be a mistake to believe that everyone who indulges the practice of shifting the blame for his actions is fated for a mental collapse. Often, usually in fact, this practice does not have so dire a consequence. But it unfits a person for a happy living. The child who has become accustomed to evading the responsibility for his acts is unprepared for the greater adjustments he must make as an adult. He is very likely to fail when he is called upon to adapt himself to the exactions of marriage and business, or to reverses of fortune. Parents and teachers should be observant of signs of this kind of compromise in children. The method of blaming uncontrollable circumstances for one's own failures is so satisfactory that it readily becomes a habit, and once it is developed it is difficult to correct. It is not difficult to prevent.

EVASION BY ILLNESS

Illness is a common means of evading responsibility and of being exonerated of effort. Many a child has been spoiled by sickness. He finds that he attracts attention and is the object of an unwonted solicitude while he is unwell. He is excused from school, he is relieved of other duties that he finds burdensome or distasteful. After his recovery, if he is confronted by some difficulty, he may try to evade it by pleading illness. When he finds that a headache wins him a holiday from school, or a release from his homework, he is tempted to gain those advantages again by a repetition of the malady. He may not be deceiving intentionally. He may, in fact, have a slight discomfort in his head, but it is not sufficient to incapacitate him; if he did not concentrate on it he would not know that he had it at all. We all have twinges and small aches of which we are unconscious while our minds are on other things, but which may become acutely painful when we think of them. The longer and more earnestly we attend to them the sharper they become.

Some mothers excuse their children's failures on the score that the youngsters were sickly in their infancy, or in their early years. When this is done in the hearing of the child, it may easily harm him. He is invited to appeal to his real or imaginary infirmities when he wishes to dispense himself from effort. He knows that this defense will be effective with his mother, he hopes it will influence the judgment of others as well. The child who has outgrown his former weaknesses need never be reminded of them. The one who continues frail should not be misled into exaggerating his fragility. On the contrary, he should be encouraged to assert himself to the limits of his strength. He ought to be trained to give as little thought to his health as prudence dictates.

It is surprising how many people avail themselves

of illness in order to escape inconvenience, or to gain some benefit. Soldiers use it to be rescued from the dangers of battle, students fall back on it in order to be granted concessions in school, some parents employ it as a net with which to hold their grown sons and daughters and thus prevent them from leaving home and leading independent lives. Hysteria manifests itself under a great variety of symptoms; the disorder may simulate almost any disease that is known to medicine. And hysteria is a defense reaction. It is the expedient of weaklings. It is a means of compelling an interest and of winning advantages which the hysteric fails to achieve by genuine accomplishments. Unlike the poet, the hysteric is not born, but made. She (for usually the hysteric is a girl or woman although men, too, fall victims to the disease) is a monument to faulty training. The patient has been positively encouraged in her unhealthy method of winning attention, or she has not been corrected of that method when she stumbled into it blindly.

The illness that is motivated or prolonged, because it is profitable, is exceedingly difficult to cure. The patient is reluctant to give up his symptoms since by doing so he would forego the advantages that they bring him. Parents and teachers must be on the watch for signs of this compromise. When they find a child who is invoking sickness as a defense mechanism kindness demands that they teach him more wholesome ways of reacting to his difficulties. It is a mistake to reward him for this kind of behavior. It is unjust to coddle a child and soften him by too much sympathy, for this line of treatment unfits him for future struggles. Of course, care must be exercised that an error is not made in the opposite direction. There must be a mean between a solicitude that is too anxious and a nonchalance that is supine. The child should most certainly be given the care that is requisite for preserving his physical health, or for restoring it when he is ill, but it is equally important that his mental soundness be safeguarded. He must not be allowed to form attitudes toward health that will cause him to refuse to face his duties manfully.

COMPARISON WITH INFERIORS

Another form of defense reaction exhibited by a fairly large number of people is that of comparing oneself with the less competent, or the less fortunate. The individual who resorts to this subterfuge admits his defeat, but he tries to minimize it. He extenuates it on the score that others are as bad as, or worse, than he. The boy who is reproached for getting a mark of only seventy-five in his classwork defends himself by replying, "Patrick Puffendorfer got only seventy-four." It is easy to form the habit of trying to buoy up one's reputation through invidious comparisons with others. The principle of relativity is not restricted to mathematics, it operates universally since all human qualities are relative. The first citizen in a small town is lost in the multitude when he moves to a great city. A boy's conduct may be model when it is contrasted with the activities of the gang in his neighborhood, but it falls far short of the behavior of his quieter brother. The child has early experience of the law of comparisons. He is repeatedly being admonished to keep his hands as clean as his sister's. He is reproached for being less obedient than the boy next door. He soon learns to employ comparisons for his own protection. When he is reproved for using slang, he says,

"I heard Dad say it." If his mother chides him for fingering the food on the table he tells her, "but you handled the tomatoes in the grocery store." He is beginning to excuse his misconduct by contrasting it favorably with the behavior of others.

The method of excusing oneself by comparisons that are derogatory to others, threatens mental health less than some of the other forms of defense reactions. Still it is harmful and repellent and, therefore, it should be discouraged. If it becomes habitual it may lead to the odious habit of gloating over the misfortunes of others. Moreover, the attitude that makes an individual satisfied with being second last is, of its nature, deadly to the spirit of initiative. For it requires only a very moderate effort to bring up the rear of the procession in the ordinary pursuits of life. That man ranks low indeed on the scale of accomplishment who cannot find someone who is inferior to himself. Hence, children should be animated with a desire to achieve within the limits of their abilities. They will thus be preserved from the emasculating habit of finding comfort in the thought that they are not the absolute last.

REFUSAL TO MEET THE ISSUE

The type of defense mechanism that is singularly objectionable is that of avoiding the battle. The attitude is observable in those dispirited people who have the feeling of "what's the use?" The danger of this particular reaction lies in the fact that the habit becomes strengthened very quickly. The individual who is disheartened by his failures, may come to feel that he cannot be worsted in the struggle, if he does not enter into it. Hence, he withdraws from the combat. It is evident that this state of mind precludes success, it makes for ultimate failure. It is true that a person may not be defeated in that precise conflict which he avoids, it is equally true that he cannot conquer in it. And it is impossible to evade *all* conflicts. Those into which we are forced will terminate badly if we have no practice in warring. The habit of refusing to take a stand against difficulties may result in a total loss of self-confidence. That is fatal. The person whose belief in himself has been undermined has taken long strides toward abnormality.

In extreme cases the habit of shirking the combat may result in negativism, a condition in which the individual becomes irresponsive to all outside stimulation. He gives no evidence that he hears when he is spoken to, he seems to be insensible to pain, he may not be influenced by even such primitive and deep-seated impulses as those of hunger and thirst. He may regress to the point where it is necessary to feed him through a tube. In a word he is completely withdrawn from reality, he is out of touch with the outside world, he has a very serious mental disease.

The injurious practice of evading the issue may start in apparently simple ways. Often, it has its beginning in school or in the home. It may first appear in the behavior of the "pouting child" who, when he is questioned, refuses to answer. The teacher may brand him as stubborn and she attempts to force him to reply, she brings pressure to bear upon him in the presence of other children. These harsh measures only accentuate his difficulty, he becomes more fearful of himself and of the situation in which he is placed.

He falls back on his customary means of protection, he becomes more silent. This is a most shortsighted refuge of safety but it is the only one he knows. When the teacher leaves him alone, and fails to call on him, because she has been unsuccessful in her efforts to bring him out of his shell, he is confirmed in his attitude of retreating.

THE STRATEGIC ROLE OF THE TEACHER

This type of child is in pressing need of treatment. The teacher should try to gain his confidence and thus find *why* he acts as he does. This process requires tact and gentleness. The child with an emotional difficulty is generally suspicious. He is likely to evade a discussion of his trouble with a stranger, especially if his feelings of fear have been aroused in school, or by the ridicule of a former teacher. The one who helps him will be animated to the patient effort demanded for the correction of his problem by this thought: if she assists him to meet his difficulties more healthily she will spare him enormous suffering. She may even save him from a final mental collapse.

CONSIGNING FAILURES TO OBLIVION

Some people attempt to save themselves from the reproach of their failures or defeats by *forgetting* them. They try to make their memory selective so that they will never recall events that are of a kind to wound their pride. When they succeed in this endeavor they spare themselves the pain of reviving the memory of past embarrassments or hardships. Unfortunately, however, it is often exceedingly difficult to forget the disagreeable, since an unpleasant event tends to live in the memory from the very fact that it was unpleasant. Situations that arouse intense feeling impress a person deeply, and as a consequence the memory of them is likely to endure. The man who uses forgetting as a defense reaction tries to *force* himself to forget and his endeavors to do this often result in queer forms of behavior. We might illustrate some of these by an example.

Let us suppose that a man goes to a distant city to attend a convention at which he is one of the speakers. When his turn to talk comes he starts off happily but in the middle of his address his memory fails him. He stumbles and falters, and finally resumes his seat in confusion, amid the painful silence of the audience. If the individual is healthy-minded, the experience may do him no serious harm. He does not enjoy references to his debacle but he tolerates them because he recognizes that his failure was real. Gradually the lapse of time and the accumulation of other interests temper the memory of his humiliation, so that he thinks of it but rarely and when he does recall it he is not made abnormally emotional by the recollection.

But he may pursue a different and a far less healthy line of tactics. In an effort to avoid further discomfiture he tries to hide the incident from others. When he returns home, he regales his friends with a description of what he saw in the city. He tells them about the convention but he makes no mention of the fiasco which he himself suffered at it. Or he may have recourse to a different method in an attempt to protect his good name. He does speak of his misadventure, but he modifies it very much in the telling. He describes it in a way that throws an air of the comic over the whole occurrence. His friends are amused by the recital, they laugh over his predicament, but, since he is the author of the joke, he is reconciled to their mirth. Or he may do this — he tells how his memory failed and how embarrassed he was but then he launched out boldly and electrified his audience by an extemporaneous discourse.

EVILS OF THE MECHANISM OF FORGETTING

All these expedients are helpful to him, if they work, but they may encounter obstacles. A fellow townsman may have been a witness to his disgrace, or a stranger who was present at it comes to town, so that the unlucky speaker is in a precarious position. There is a real danger that both his original experience and the dishonest means he used to cloak it will be revealed, to his discredit. It is then that his conduct may become peculiar.

He may become violent in his criticism of conventions. He raves against them as a vast waste of time, they accomplish no practical good, they result only in a series of useless resolutions, they impose the necessity of listening to interminable and tedious speeches. He may conceive an abnormal dislike for crowds, he cannot bear to be in a large hall, he is intensely uncomfortable in church or in a theater. He excuses himself from attendance at public gatherings for reasons that impress others as inconclusive. The singular thing is that his emotional reaction is out of all proportion to its immediate cause. In reality, he is not responding to the situation in which he finds himself at present, he is aroused by it because of its resemblance to the setting in which he experienced the humiliation that he would like to forget.

The Danger of Defense Mechanism

DISCLAIMING PERSONAL DEFECTS

Refusing to admit a defect, or a fault, is a familiar kind of defense reaction. This method may be effective, provided that the imperfection is not too glaring. When, however, a person's deficiency is marked, or when he is constantly being reminded of it, he cannot continue to blind himself to the facts. Then he may fall back on another expedient. He criticizes his critic; he becomes angry with the one who blames him; he proceeds to point out some flaw in his accuser. This is a practical weapon for self-protection, it places the attacker on the defensive. He is put to the necessity of vindicating himself and hence his attention is diverted from the criticism that he was venturing.

But this method is at best a temporary benefit to the one who employs it. It serves only to relieve him of the present attack, he is still open to future criticisms, or reproaches, for his shortcomings. It is hard to acknowledge unflattering truths about oneself but if they are facts they must be faced. The rational and healthy course to pursue is to correct the failings that may become causes of conflict, and the first step toward their correction is the confession of their existence. If a person cannot mend a defect, if for instance he suffers from some physical blemish that attracts unwelcome attention, the sane thing for him to do is to accept his deficiency and to make the best of it. More abnormal behavior results from trying to cover up some peculiarity that cannot be concealed than would ever follow from its calm admission.

Children need guidance in learning to admit their irremediable handicaps, whatever form these may take.

The most effective means of helping them in this task is to teach them how to compensate for their particular defects. Briefly, the process of compensation consists in substituting attainable desires for those that can never be reached, either because of the individual's physical or mental limitations, or because of the nature of the circumstances in which he is placed. If he succeeds in making this adjustment he will be spared the pain that he would experience were he to ambition achievements or possessions which, to him, are impossible. We shall speak at length of the mechanism of compensation in the following chapter.

EXPLAINING AWAY DEFEAT

Another form of self-justification that is likely to interfere with a well-balanced personality is rationalization. It is a sort of intellectual defense reaction and is one of the most common of the methods employed to palliate one's failures, or to excuse one's defects. There are few people who have not had recourse to this type of defense mechanism at some time or other.

Rationalization consists in the attempt to explain one's actions on the basis of reasonable motives. The reasons that are adduced are not actually responsible for the bit of behavior in question, but they are proffered because they are deemed more acceptable than are the true causes of the action. An instance of rationalization is seen in the behavior of the person, who feels that his conduct has been actuated by selfish or ignoble impulses, and who is unwilling to admit that fact. He lays great stress, therefore, on some more worthy motive which, in reality, may have played but a very slight part in determining his action. The reasons that he advances, in his effort to avoid reproach, or to win social approval, may be exceedingly plausible, often the rationalizer himself is half persuaded of their validity. As a matter of fact, however, the motive that he puts forward is not the cause of his conduct, rather it is the effect of it. Because he has acted in such a way that he feels the need of protecting himself, he thinks back over his conduct in order to find an explanation that may satisfy his critics.

THE TEMPTATION TO RATIONALIZE

Public opinion is likely to frown down upon behavior that is prompted by mere sentiment or emotion, hence we are desirous of convincing others that our conduct is the result of thoughtful consideration rather than the outcome of caprice or whims. The child soon learns, from the treatment he receives, that he cannot adequately defend his actions by ascribing them to his feelings. In other words, experience teaches him that it is not satisfactory to say that he did a thing because he wanted to do it. Were he to give such an answer when he is questioned about his conduct he would be punished for impudence. So he does not advance such an excuse, rather he casts about for an explanation that is likely to prove expedient. When he is asked why he is late for school he says that his mother failed to call him on time, or the clock was slow, or he missed a car. These statements may be true but they do not give the real cause of his tardiness, if he had hurried a little he could have been in ample time for class. Were the boy perfectly candid he would tell the teacher, "I hate school so I came as slowly as I could." He loitered along the way in order to delay his distasteful duty to the latest possible moment. But he cannot afford to broadcast this truth since such a frank explanation of his delinquency would work a hardship on him. Instead he tries to make his questioner believe that his late arrival is due to causes for which he is not responsible and for which he should not be blamed.

Rationalization is not an outright lie, rather it is a distortion of the truth, it is an instance of misplaced emphasis. Usually many factors co-operate to influence our conduct so that we may offer several explanations for almost anything we do. A person may study mental hygiene because he needs credits for his degree, or because he wants the information that the course imparts, or because he is interested in the matter, or because he regards the subject as a "snap course." The rationalizer singles out that particular motive which he judges most seemly in a given situation. When he is successful in his attempt — and some people acquire a remarkable dexterity in rationalizing — he distracts the attention of possible critics from the true cause of his conduct and thus he escapes their censure.

RATIONALIZING, A COMMON PHENOMENON

Rationalization is an outstanding symptom in certain grave mental diseases; the paranoic invokes it to protect himself from feelings of guilt or to salve his wounded pride, or to solace himself for frustrated hopes.[2] This type of defense mechanism is also fre-

[2]Paranoia is the term used to designate the mental disease that is characterized by systematic and fixed delusions. These take many forms but they are all expressions of a very self-centered personality and, usually, they develop into ideas of persecution. True paranoia is a rare disease, but there are many disorders that resemble it in some ways, and which, therefore, are called paranoid states. The term means "like paranoia."

quently found in melancholia. But rationalization is not a prerogative of those who are mentally deranged; it is most extensively utilized by people who are rated as normal and we encounter instances of it wherever we turn. The boy who has stolen an apple from the grocer and who therefore fears to meet the man, sets up a barrage of arguments when his mother wants him to go to the store — it is raining, he has just recovered from a cold, he is afraid of contracting another. The lazy student excuses his poor marks on the score that he was not feeling well on the day of examination, he had slept little the night before, his head ached, he simply could not concentrate. The athlete who is called from the game by the coach because of his unsatisfactory playing limps painfully as he makes his way to the bench. These are but examples of the countless means by which individuals attempt to defend themselves against reproach or to win lenient judgments on their conduct.

The dangers of rationalization are so obvious that we need scarcely delay to describe them. In extreme cases the habit may lead to serious delusions, but even in its milder forms the practice is destructive of wholesome, balanced personality. It makes for intellectual dishonesty, it is a genuine obstacle in the way of achievement. The individual who discovers that his skill in rationalizing protects him from the consequences of his failures is deprived of a great stimulus to effort. He is likely to grow lazy and careless and inactive. The child must be safeguarded against the hurtful habit of making excuses instead of "making good." The need for training children to a truthful acknowledgment of their faults of omission and commission is accentuated by two facts; the first is that children manifest a widespread tendency to rationalize, and secondly, they see examples of the process in many of the adults with whom they are thrown in contact.

CPSIA information can be obtained
at www.ICGtesting.com
Printed in the USA
BVHW031837130720
583640BV00001B/63